# BRITISH EGYPTOLOGY

# BRITISH
# EGYPTOLOGY
## *1549–1906*

## By
## John David Wortham

DAVID & CHARLES: NEWTON ABBOT

ISBN 0 7153 5545 7

Printed in Great Britain by
Lowe & Brydone (Printers) Limited
for David & Charles (Publishers) Limited
South Devon House, Newton Abbot, Devon

*This book is for Dena and David*

# Preface

A MAJOR occupation of modern British intellectual history has been the exploration of the ancient civilizations of the Near East, particularly that of Egypt. Until now, however, there has been no scholarly and comprehensive study of the development of Egyptology in Great Britain. A few students have written erudite accounts of the evolution of specific aspects of Egyptological studies, and there is one general history. The many popular accounts—of which C. W. Ceram's *Gods, Graves, and Scholars* is the best known—make very entertaining reading but present somewhat incomplete and distorted outlines of the evolution of Egyptology.

The most common distortion results from near-exclusive concentration on nineteenth-century discoveries. Most writers open their accounts of the "rise" of Egyptology with the work of the French savants in 1798–1800. After describing the work of the Napoleonic expedition, they quickly move on to discuss Jean François Champollion's decipherment of the hieroglyphic writing. Leaving Champollion, they move to later archaeological work. Rarely do any of these writers attempt to consider the exploration of Egypt before 1798.

Actually, educated Europeans had always shown a strong interest in the antiquities and civilization of ancient Egypt. In the works of classical geographers and historians Europeans had found much material on Egypt. The biblical stories about the Israelites' sojourn in Egypt provided a constant source of interest in that ancient land. Beginning in the early sixteenth century, European travelers published descriptions of Egypt's antiquities. The first objects described were the obelisks that Roman emperors had transported from Egypt and erected in Rome and Constantinople. Later travelers described the obelisks at Alexandria and Heliopolis, as well as the pyramids at Giza and other places near Cairo. By 1750, European explorers had published accurate diagrams, drawings, and plans of all the temples, obelisks, tombs, and pyramids that stretched along the Nile from Alexandria to the first cataract at Aswân. A few of these early explorers had even penetrated beyond Aswân into Nubia and away from the Nile to Lake Moeris in the Faiyûm region. The French savants who explored the ruins of Egypt from 1798 to 1801 were not able to improve on the descriptions of the Nile ruins given by the earlier travelers.

Standard histories of archaeology include little information about the study by Europeans of ancient Egyptian writing before Champollion's work. Once most writers describe Champollion's decipherment of the hieroglyphic writing, they drop the subject. The reader is left to assume, perhaps, that the new phonetic system of hieroglyphic decipherment introduced by Thomas Young and Champollion met with instant acceptance. No more distorted impression of the decipherment could exist. Actually, the decipherment resulted from a long and varied process. Before scholars could make any progress toward unlocking the Egyptian inscriptions, two developments had to occur. First, the predominant Neoplatonic theories about the hieroglyphs had to be discredited, and, second, scholars had to acquire accurate copies of the Egyptian inscriptions. By 1750 speculative thinkers were criticizing the older concept of the hieroglyphs, and travelers had begun to copy the hieroglyphic inscriptions that they found on Egyptian monuments. The work of these earlier men made Champollion's decipherment possible.

The general acceptance of the new system did not come easily. At first many scholars rejected it outright. Later, scholars began to doubt the usefulness of the new system because the translation of Egyptian inscriptions proceeded very slowly. Only in the latter half of the nineteenth century did the study of the ancient Egyptian writing produce incontestable proof that it could supply useful data to historians, students of literature, and scholars interested in ancient religions.

The popular histories of Egyptology rarely bother to recount the discovery of the prehistoric cultures in Egypt, and, if they do, they always concentrate on the post-1894 activities of Sir Flinders Petrie. Earlier explorers of Egypt's prehistory receive no attention. Alexander Henry Rhind, an early archaeologist, discovered a prehistoric grave in Egypt in the early 1850's. In the 1870's Sir John Lubbock went hunting for prehistoric flints in Egypt. By the time Petrie appeared there, the earlier discoveries by Rhind, Lubbock, and other explorers had already stimulated great interest in the prehistory of Egypt. Appreciating the work of these earlier explorers does not, however, detract in any way from the importance of Petrie's discoveries.

Finally, the standard accounts of the history of Egyptology devote too little space to the evolution of archaeological methodology before the arrival of Petrie in Egypt.

Specifically, the work of Rhind in establishing more exacting standards for excavation merits greater attention than it has received.

In this history of British Egyptology, I attempt to show how some of the distorted historical conceptions were corrected by presenting a survey of the evolution of this discipline in Great Britain. I selected 1906 as a convenient terminal date because in that year Petrie finished the last of his excavations among the prehistoric and early dynastic tombs at Abydos. His excavations there gave final proof of the growth of Egypt's dynastic civilization from earlier prehistoric cultures. This demonstration marked the end of an era in Egyptian archaeology.

A major problem in my research was relating British exploration in Egypt with that of Americans, French, Germans, and Italians. Although there is a history of American Egyptology, it is inadequately researched, and much must be done before the historian can evaluate the relative importance of each country's contributions. Nevertheless, I have rendered some tentative judgments of this nature.

A number of scholarly books were particularly useful in my research. Warren Royal Dawson has provided historians with an invaluable guide to Near Eastern travelers and scholars in his *Who Was Who in Egyptology*. In *The Myth of Egypt and Its Hieroglyphs in European Tradition*, Erik Iversen presents the best account of the steps leading to the decipherment of the Egyptian writing. Louis Greener's *The Discovery of Egypt* appeared too late to aid me in my research, but it is a very competent description of the general development of Egyptology.

At this point I wish to express my gratitude for the aid given by a number of people. The present text and format of this work have profited greatly from the suggestions of George Basalla, of the University of Texas, and Ray Mathis, of Georgia Southern College. William Goetzmann, Archibald Ross Lewis, and Stanford Eugene Lehmberg, all of the University of Texas, read my manuscript carefully. The Research Committee of Georgia Southern College, under the chairmanship of Donald A. Olewine, financed the securing of illustrations with a grant.

JOHN DAVID WORTHAM

*Birmingham, Alabama*
*January 15, 1971*

# Contents

# Illustrations

*British Egyptology, 1549–1906*

An Egyptian nobleman hunting and fishing
"Chase of the Hippopotamus"
"Joseph Interpreting Pharaoh's Dream"
"Embalming the Body of Joseph"

# Maps

# BRITISH EGYPTOLOGY

# I

# Egyptology During the Renaissance

URING the three centuries that preceded the decipherment of Egyptian hieroglyphic writing in the 1820's, knowledge of ancient Egyptian civilization and history was mostly limited to the information contained in certain of the writings of classical antiquity. A central theme of this book is the demise of the classical idea of what the ancient nation along the Nile was like and its replacement by modern concepts based on original Egyptian sources. Before the gradual breakdown of the earlier view of Egypt is considered, it is necessary to examine the visualization of ancient Egyptian culture in the works of some sixteenth- and seventeenth-century English writers. To understand their view, it is necessary, in turn, to examine the sources from which they learned about Egypt.

If a Renaissance scholar needed facts for a dissertation on ancient Egypt, or a Renaissance traveler sought information about Egyptian "antiquities," he had to seek it primarily in non-Egyptian sources. The only Egyptian source available was the literature of the medieval Copts. In addition to the Coptic literature, he might consult the writings of the classi-

3

cal historians, geographers, and literary figures, certain works in Arabic and Syrian, the biblical writings, some medieval sources, contemporary monographs on various aspects of Egyptian civilization and geography, and travelers' descriptions of the Egyptian antiquities. For the most part the English researcher was restricted to the biblical and classical sources and the contemporary accounts of scholars and travelers. Throughout the Renaissance the works of the classical writers continued to be the most important source of information concerning the geography, antiquities, and religion of the ancient Egyptians.[1]

The great literary works of Greece and Rome made available a vast amount of information pertaining to the ancient civilization of Egypt. Herodotus described in great detail the landscapes, animals, and plants that he found along the Nile. His narrative also contains discussions of Egyptian religion, the hieroglyphic system of writing, and the better-known Greek and native monuments. The geographical writings of Strabo provided much detailed information on the pyramids, temples, and tombs of Egypt. The first five books of the *Bibliotheca* of Diodorus Siculus described Egyptian ruins.[2]

Plutarch's *Isis and Osiris* was the most detailed account of ancient Egyptian religion available in England during the Renaissance. In the works of Plutarch's contemporary, Flavius Josephus, Renaissance historians found many excerpts, including a list of Egyptian kings, from the most important ancient book on Egypt, Manetho's history of Egypt. Pliny's *Natural History* contained descriptions of monuments in Egypt and the Egyptian obelisks that the emperors had brought to Rome. The *Roman History* of Ammianus Marcellinus was another important Renaissance source for factual data about the obelisks in Rome, the antiquities of the Nile Valley, the mysterious hieroglyphs, and the terrain, plants, and animals of Egypt.[3]

Much of the information that these ancient writers supplied was accurate, but much was also erroneous, confusing, and misleading. Plato, Ammianus Marcellinus, and other classical authors advanced the theory—now known to be wrong—that Egypt was the land in which man had first developed art, religion, and science and gave many examples to "prove" that the early Greeks received their first acquaintance with these matters from Egyptian priests.[4] Medieval and Renaissance works—many of which purported to be of ancient origin—reinforced the belief that Egypt was the original homeland of the pursuit of knowledge.

For data on Egyptian civilization Renaissance writers often turned to the church fathers. Clement of Alexandria described the hieroglyphic system of writing, and Eusebius commented adversely on the religion of the ancient Egyptians. It is partly from the works of Eusebius that ancient Egypt gained a reputation for having been the source of pagan superstition and fanaticism.[5]

Sometime before 1171, Rabbi Benjamin of Tudela visited Egypt and, after his return, published a widely read description of the Nile Valley. His book was filled with errors, many of which persisted into the seventeenth century. These errors included the mislocating of the biblical city of Pithom; an attempt to identify the ruins of Memphis with Mizraim, another Old Testament city; his belief that the Pyramids of Giza were granaries that the Hebrews had built; and his opinion that a hieroglyph-covered obelisk in Alexandria had served as a tomb. Clearly Benjamin lacked any appreciation of the structure and function of obelisks and pyramids.[6]

The medieval writings attributed to the Egyptian king Hermes Trismegistus exerted a great influence upon the Renaissance idea of ancient Egyptian religion. Scholars believed not only that Hermes had actually lived but that the Platonic content of the works attributed to him revealed the religious beliefs of the ancient Egyptians. Two important English students of the Hermetic works were John Dee, Queen Elizabeth's astrologer, and John Everard, a seventeenth-century translator of these works.[7]

Sir John Mandeville, the author of a travel book that was a popular work throughout the sixteenth and seventeenth centuries, discussed hieroglyphic writing and the pyramids. Mandeville, who lived during the fourteenth century, repeated the mistaken belief that the pyramids were Hebrew-built granaries and explicitly rejected the idea that they could be tombs. According to his reasoning, the pyramids could not be tombs because tombs were not hollow, and the pyramids, he assured the reader, were hollow, a belief that lasted into the late nineteenth century.[8] English writers, however, did not follow Mandeville but instead correctly considered the pyramids to be tombs.

Italian books of the fifteenth and early sixteenth centuries influenced English thought on Egypt. Among these works were the widely read histories of Annius, or Giovanni Nanni, a Dominican abbot and classical scholar of the fifteenth century. Annius claimed to have discovered twelve lost historical works, including the Egyptian history by Manetho. All of them were clever forgeries, but throughout the sixteenth and seventeenth centuries English scholars for the most part accepted Annius' works and his account of Egyptian history as genuine.[9]

Annius had to be read in the Latin, but there was an Elizabethan translation of another work by an Italian, the *Hypnerotomachia Poliphili* of the Dominican friar Francesco Colonna. This work is an allegory in which obelisks, pyramids, and hieroglyphs appear as symbols. Colonna's descriptions of these objects undoubtedly influenced the educated Englishman's concept of them.[10]

The interpretation of the hieroglyphs prevailing in Renaissance England came largely from the works of fifteenth- and sixteenth-century foreign authors. The most famous of these works was the extremely popular *Hieroglyphics* of Horapollo, which first appeared early in the sixteenth century. Other foreign writers on this subject widely read in England were Pierius Valerianus, whose chief work on hieroglyphs appeared in 1556, Leone Battista Alberti, an architect who stressed the need to use hieroglyphic "symbols" in inscriptions, and Herwarth von Hohenburg, author of *Thesaurus Hieroglyphicarum*. The two famous Renaissance scholars Erasmus and John Reuchlin also published works on hieroglyphic writing. Andrea Alciati, who issued his *Emblemata* in 1531 at Augsburg, became the founder of the emblematic genre of literature. Emblematic literature flourished in sixteenth- and seventeenth-century England, and the English writers continued Alciati's practice of deriving many emblems from hieroglyphs.[11]

Travel narratives by Leo Africanus, a Roman Catholic cleric and papal scholar, and Pierre Belon, a French explorer, described the ruins along the Nile's banks. Both men had visited Egypt during the first half of the sixteenth century, and Leo had traveled all the way to Aswân and the First Cataract. English readers found in his work a fairly recent description of ruins which other Europeans would not see for a century and a half.[12]

Early in the seventeenth century Athanasius Kircher, a German scholar, published a number of controversial works on the Egyptian systems of writing. Kircher had obtained some notable results from his study of Coptic, but, unfortunately, too many scholars accepted as equally valid his "translations" of the hieroglyphs.[13]

From the works of ancient, medieval, and Renaissance travelers and scholars, the Englishmen of the sixteenth and seventeenth centuries formed a picture of the Egyptian antiquities that was often accurate in physical detail but inaccurate historically. They had only the inaccurate classical sources and erroneous or forged contemporary documents to rely upon for the history of ancient Egypt. Hence, they produced exotic, totally misleading accounts of ancient Egyptian culture and civilization.

The way in which this lack of reliable historical information led commentators astray is seen in their ready acceptance of numerous fraudulent Christian antiquities that the Arabs exhibited to every traveler in Cairo. These "antiquities" were shrines that the Arabs, who probably accepted the old stories about these places, insisted marked the places where the Holy Family had rested after their flight to Egypt. Since Renaissance writers believed in the literal truth of biblical stories, they naturally viewed favorably the travelers' reports of these Christian "antiquities." Although these commentators accepted uncritically individual reports about Christian antiquities in Egypt, they were skeptical of contemporary information about pyramids, obelisks, and other pre-Christian objects.[14]

Ancient Egypt had contained two of the Seven Wonders of the World, the Pharos, the lighthouse near Alexandria, and the Pyramids of Giza.[15] In the sixteenth and seventeenth centuries only the Pyramids of Giza were still standing, but writers assured their readers that these Egyptian structures were far more wonderful than the fabulous animals and objects travelers to other parts of the world described.[16] Among the antiquities of Egypt the Pyramids continued to hold the center of attention until eighteenth- and nineteenth-century travelers brought back detailed accounts and drawings of the large ruins in Upper Egypt.

Many Renaissance Englishmen had peculiar ideas of the general shape of an Egyptian pyramid. Writers used the terms "pyramid" and "obelisk" interchangeably, and as a consequence accounts of pyramids in histories and popular literature often pictured them as large obelisks. In his history of the Turkish Empire, Richard Knolles, relying on the latest travelers' accounts, described the pyramid as having a "lower tower" and a "spire." Shakespeare, after perusing the same authorities, put a window in one of his pyramids, and Christopher Marlowe indicated that he believed the pyramids to be hollow.[17]

Confusion about the purpose for which the Egyptians had constructed the pyramids was not as widespread as mistaken ideas about their shape. A few authors continued the medieval concept of the pyramids as "Joseph's granaries," but most agreed with Herodotus that the Egyptian kings had erected the pyramids as sepulchers to hold their embalmed bodies. The descriptions of how the Egyptians built the pyramids came from Herodotus and other ancients and thus perpetuated both the accuracies and the errors of these writers.[18]

Other Egyptian antiquities provoked interest among Renaissance writers, but none as much as the pyramids. Geographers attempted to find the location of the Pharos and the sites of the ancient biblical and Greek towns of Tanis, Ramses, Pithom, and Daphnae. The ruins on the island in Lake Moeris appeared on Renaissance maps—as pyramids, which, of course, they are not—and the ruins of Memphis and the mummy tombs thereabouts attracted some attention.[19] By the end of the seventeenth century English travelers had published detailed and accurate drawings of the Pyramids at Giza, but it was not until the mid-eighteenth century that detailed accounts of other Egyptian ruins were available.

Historically unreliable source materials, including the Bible, hampered scholarly discussion of ancient Egyptian culture and civilization. The story of the confrontation of Moses and Aaron with the Egyptian magicians at Pharaoh's court convinced many scholars that the Egyptians had been witches and sorcerers, and even the inventors of magic. The

Hermetic works, which described the philosophers' stone, and the belief that Moses had learned from the Egyptian priests how to transmute base metals into gold convinced many writers that alchemy had originated in ancient Egypt.[20] The idea of the ancient Egyptians as enchanters, magicians, and alchemists received additional support from the theories then current concerning the nature of Egyptian hieroglyphic writing.

Classical and Renaissance writers believed that hiero-glyphic writing had no relation to any ordinary form of graphic writing based on words and letters. Instead, it was thought to be a special kind of symbolic writing in which the hieroglyphs might appear to be pictures of common animals and objects but actually were mystical symbols. Each hieroglyph, if properly understood, revealed some-thing about the true essence of things. Only one adept in Neoplatonic philosophy could ever hope to understand the hieroglyphs, but the reward for achieving this feat would be the direct confrontation of the human mind with divine ideas. This concept of hieroglyphic writing—erroneous and terribly misleading—dominated all speculation about the hieroglyphs until the mid-eighteenth century.[21]

The Egyptian practice of embalming attracted much at-tention during the Renaissance. Herodotus, Diodorus Sicu-lus, and Pliny all described, in greater or lesser detail, the process by which the ancient Egyptians had mummified bodies. Many scholars believed incorrectly that the Egyp-tians had developed mummification out of a belief in the transmigration of souls. Since scholars considered Egypt to be the original source of all wisdom, including the doctrines of the Pythagoreans, this did not seem an unlikely explana-tion of the practice of embalming.

Although there were very few complete mummies avail-able, many Englishmen of the sixteenth and seventeenth centuries had seen pieces of mummies. Doctors often prescribed "mummy" as medicine to cure excessive bleeding, bruises, wounds, and similar bodily ailments. The idea of taking as medicine part of an embalmed body that had lain in the ground for centuries repulsed Robert Boyle, the pioneer chemist, who regarded the practice as cannibalism. Nevertheless, mummy was a standard item in many apothecary shops, a fact that Sir Thomas Browne took note of when he wrote, "Mummie is become Merchandise, Mizraim cures wounds, and Pharaoh is sold for balsams."[22]

Reliable sources upon which historians could base a history of Egypt did not exist; nevertheless, throughout this period they attempted to write Egyptian history. The sketch of Egyptian history included in Sir Walter Ralegh's *History of the World* typifies very well these early efforts. Ralegh relied on the classical writers, the Bible, the forgeries of such writers as Annius, and contemporary travel narratives for his "facts" about Egyptian history. The result was a chronicle that was almost totally unhistoric. Ralegh inserted many mythical kings in his outline of Egyptian history. He treated the biblical stories about the Hebrews in Egypt as incontestable truth, and he accepted as historical fact many legendary events. The *History of the World* was more accurate in those parts in which Ralegh described the physical remains of ancient Egypt, where he made use of modern explorers' accounts. Even there, however, he made serious errors of interpretation. At one point, Ralegh, instead of following Belon, who had correctly stated that the Pyramids of Giza were royal tombs, insisted that the Egyptians had erected the structures as astronomical observatories like the ziggurats of Babylonia. Ralegh's work must be considered a brave attempt to write a universal history with the poor materials then available, but the section on Egypt reveals how hopeless at that time the task of writing accurate ancient history was.[23]

# II

# English Travelers
in Egypt
During the Renaissance

O departure from the classical conception of Egyptian civilization was likely to occur as long as scholars were studying about it only in very old books. Progress began to be made toward assembling a more accurate picture of Egypt only when travelers started bringing back and publishing detailed reports of Egyptian monuments they had actually seen. The earliest of these travelers were tourists, agents of trading companies, and a very few scholars and scientists. The first Egyptian monuments that Englishmen visited and described, however, were not those in Egypt but the large number of Egyptian obelisks brought to Rome by the emperors. They had placed the obelisks in prominent places in the city. All but one had been pushed over by invaders during the Middle Ages. In the years 1585 to 1589, Pope Sixtus V had important obelisks erected again, an event that attracted attention throughout Europe. These tall objects, covered with the mysterious hieroglyphs, commanded many major avenues in Rome. There was also a large tomb in Rome, known as the Pyramid of Cestius that greatly influenced the European idea of a

pyramid's structure during the Renaissance and even until the nineteenth century.

In 1549, William Thomas published in his *The History of Italy* the first description in English of the obelisks and the "pyramid" in Rome. Throughout the next two centuries many other travelers published detailed accounts of the Roman obelisks. Authors of guidebooks for travelers in Italy referred frequently to these great stone needles. One English nobleman contemplated buying an obelisk and transporting it to London, but technical difficulties proved too great. Later, when other Englishmen had begun to visit and describe the ancient sites in Egypt, the best descriptions of hieroglyphs often still came from observations of those on the Roman obelisks.[1]

Beginning with Lawrence Aldersey, an otherwise unknown Elizabethan traveler who journeyed to Egypt in the year 1586–87, English travelers began to publish descriptions of the ruins they had observed in Egypt.[2] Aldersey mentioned seeing the column and obelisk then known as Pompey's Pillar and Pharaoh's Needle in Alexandria, the three Pyramids at Giza, and the ruins of Memphis near Cairo, but he made no more than a brief, passing comment on each of these ruins.

The following year another traveler whose history is obscure today, John Evesham, visited Giza. Evesham noted that only the largest of the three pyramids, the Great Pyramid, had an entrance, and by torchlight he explored its ascending passage and the so-called King's Chamber, where he saw what was later identified as the emptied sarcophagus of Cheops (Khufu), the builder of the pyramid.

John Sanderson, a commercial agent for the Turkey Company, spent some eighteen months, from October, 1585, to March, 1587, in Egypt. Sanderson visited the ancient sites in Alexandria, at Giza, and at Memphis, and he published the first descriptions of the necropolis on the eastern side

EGYPT

Reprinted from Sir Alan Gardiner, *Egypt of the Pharaohs: An Introduction,*
Oxford, The Clarendon Press, 1962.

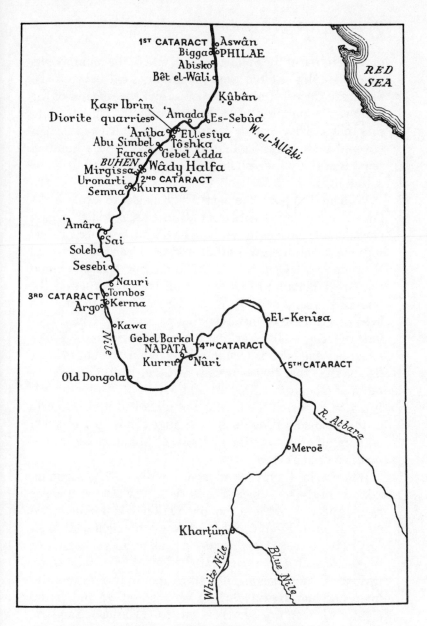

## NUBIA AND THE SUDAN

Reprinted from Sir Alan Gardiner, *Egypt of the Pharaohs: An Introduction,*
Oxford, The Clarendon Press, 1962.

of Alexandria, of the Sphinx at Giza, and of the mummy pits near Memphis. At the time he saw it, sand covered the Sphinx to the neck, hiding the paws and the remains of the temple. The mummy pits consisted of tombs cut back into rock cliffs. They had been filled with embalmed bodies covered with cloth. Sanderson shipped some six hundred pounds of this preserved flesh of long-dead Egyptians to be sold as medicine in England.

William Lithgow, the next Englishman to explore the Giza Plateau, arrived there in 1612. Lithgow later gained considerable fame as the author of a narrative of his wanderings and adventures in Europe and the Near East. Like all the other early visitors to Giza, he felt compelled to climb the Great Pyramid to its apex, and later he explored the interior passages and rooms. His narrative, which contains brief descriptions of the ascending passage, the Grand Gallery, the King's Chamber, and the sarcophagus in the King's Chamber, includes as well the first general account in English of the other two pyramids at Giza, later identified as those of Chephren (Khafre) and Mycerinus (Menkaure). Lithgow discussed the Sphinx but identified it erroneously as the Colossus of Memnon (the huge statue that classical authors referred to as the Colossus of Memnon lay farther up the Nile at Thebes).

Interest in Egypt developed rapidly in the opening decades of the seventeenth century. A new class of traveler soon appeared on the scene, one who would dominate the exploration of Egypt until the end of the eighteenth century. This traveler was usually a well-to-do gentleman or the son of such a gentleman. He had an excellent education in classical languages and literature; the study of Arabic also interested him. He traveled up the Nile to Giza and, in the eighteenth century, farther on to Dahshûr, Saqqara, Thebes, and Aswân. He took detailed notes and made careful drawings. The results of his investigations appeared in book form soon after he returned home. His interest in antiquities was general, including those of England. Such a traveler gradually turned the trip to Egypt,—formerly either a business journey or an extension of the grand tour—into a serious archaeological expedition.

The voyage of George Sandys to Egypt in 1610 marked the appearance of such a gentleman-traveler on the scene. Sandys was to win some distinction as a translator of Ovid's *Metamorphoses*, and he also served for a time as an official in the new colony of Virginia. All that, however, still lay in the future when he went to Egypt in 1610. In addition to his excellent classical education, Sandys was deeply interested in the new scientific knowledge of the age, particularly geology. In preparation for his trip to the Middle East he had read all the major works on the subject.[3]

At the end of January, 1611, Sandys arrived at Alexandria. After exploring its ruins, he traveled up the Nile to Cairo and then went on to Giza. He first directed his attention to the Great Pyramid. The massive stone blocks the Egyptians had used in its construction caused him to marvel at the skill of the builders. The heat of the pyramid's unventilated interior forced Sandys, as it did practically every visitor before the twentieth century, to disrobe and enter the pyramid virtually naked. Besides the passages and rooms noted by earlier travelers, Sandys described the entrance to the "well," a large hole near the end of the ascending passage that leads to passages deep within the massive stone foundation. Sandys visited the Queen's Chamber and the King's Chamber and, above the latter, discovered the relieving chambers (built to take the enormous weight of the pyramid's upper portions off the roof of the King's Chamber). He appears to have been the last traveler for over a century to take note of the relieving chambers. Sandys, like many other explorers, commented on the foul odor that filled the interior of the pyramid.

c

The second and third pyramids of Giza and the Sphinx also attracted Sandys' attention. The Egyptians, he correctly asserted, had cut the Sphinx out of the desert rock. The Sphinx was not unique; he had seen many smaller ones among Egyptian ruins. Beyond Giza lay the pyramids at Dahshûr and Saqqara. Sandys could see them in the distance and realized that up close they would appear just as large as the Pyramids of Giza.

Although he was not able to visit the mummy pits, Sandys examined many mummies in Cairo. They were wrapped in cloth which, when removed, revealed each member of the body to be intact but blackened by age. In his book Sandys described the inscriptions written on paper and the small metal and stone statuettes of the Egyptian gods found in the mummies' stomachs.

Sandys' *Travels* proved to be a very popular book, appearing in nine separate editions during the course of the seventeenth century. It was packed with classical lore on Egyptian antiquities, but the best parts of the book are Sandys' own descriptions of the things he saw. Most of the more interesting antiquities in the Upper Nile Valley had, of course, lain beyond the area of his explorations, but Sandys brought back from Giza the first realistic drawings of the Pyramids of Giza, those in the distance at Dahshûr and Saqqara, and the Sphinx.

Another gentleman-traveler, whose accounts of Egyptian antiquities compared favorably with those of Sandys, was Henry Blount, who visited Egypt in 1634 while on the grand tour. Blount published his account, *A Voyage into the Levant*, in 1636. By 1671 it had passed through eight editions, and a German translation appeared in 1687.

In Alexandria, Blount observed Cleopatra's Needle, a large hieroglyph-covered obelisk lying in the sand piles along the waterfront, as well as Pharoah's Needle, a standing obelisk. He also visited the Pyramids of Giza and the mummy pits near Thebes, and he spent much of his time at the pyramids at Dahshûr and Saqqara. These pyramids were very similar to those at Giza, except that they were further disintegrated and had no steps. Blount became the first Englishman to venture out into the Faiyûm, where he visited the ruins of a structure which classical writers had misnamed the Labyrinth but which was really a temple belonging to the reign of Amenemhet III of the Twelfth Dynasty.[4]

In 1646, John Greaves, a professor of astronomy and mathematics in the University of Oxford, published a work called *Pyramidographia: Or a Description of the Pyramids in Aegypt*. In addition to being the first treatise by an Englishman concerned solely with describing the monuments of Egypt, the *Pyramidographia* is the first scientific study of the Egyptian pyramids.[5]

Unlike the other Englishmen who had visited Egypt and described its antiquities, Greaves entered Egypt with very definite scientific aims in mind. While the general appearance of the Pyramids had often been described, no explorer had taken exact measurements of either the interior or the exterior features. Greaves intended to supply this information by going to Giza and measuring the Pyramids with scientific instruments. This he proceeded to do on two visits to the Giza Plateau during the winter of 1637–38.

Greaves took careful measurements of the exterior of the Great Pyramid and observed the arrangement of the stone blocks. He climbed to the top, noted that erosion by the weather had damaged many of the stone blocks, and then measured the small flat area on its top. Then, holding a lighted taper in his hand, he entered the pyramid. Large numbers of huge bats made their home in its passages and chambers. He proceeded down the entrance passage to the "well," lowered a line into it, and dropped some flaming material into it to try to estimate its depth. The rubbish of centuries had almost completely clogged it.

From the well Greaves headed straight on to the Queen's Chamber. He took careful measurements of the room and noted an empty niche in which he correctly guessed that a statue had once stood, but the unpleasant odor of the chamber soon drove him out. Next he walked up the Grand Gallery to the King's Chamber, noting the grooved stone benches lining the sides of the passageway. He accurately surmised that the benches had once possessed a nonornamental purpose, but he had no way of knowing what has since been ascertained: that these structures had been used in sealing off the ascending passage. He also measured the short passage that led into the King's Chamber.

The King's Chamber proved to be a magnificently beautiful room. Huge stone beams supported the roof, and a sarcophagus rested on the floor. In order to examine the stone of the sarcophagus more closely, he broke a piece off. Greaves suggested that the sarcophagus, whose size and weight precluded its having been brought up the passageways, must have been placed in position before the builders roofed over the King's Chamber.

In all, Greaves spent a very profitable three hours within the Great Pyramid. The diagram that he drew of it provided the first really accurate picture of its interior structure. Ancient writers, who had never ventured inside it, had stated that hieroglyphs covered its interior. Greaves exploded this myth when he stated that the Great Pyramid was devoid of hieroglyphs. Still, much of the Great Pyramid remained unexplored, because Greaves did not have the equipment to descend the well into the subterranean passages and chamber.

Greaves did not examine the pyramids of Chephren and Mycerinus in detail. The sides of Chephren's pyramid were

smoother than those of the other pyramids, he observed, and
the exterior of Mycerinus' tomb was covered with white
stone rather than the black marble mentioned by other
writers. It was impossible to enter either pyramid.

In addition to the three at Giza, Greaves mentioned having seen about twenty other pyramids in Egypt, including
the great Step Pyramid at Saqqara. But he did not go up
the Nile farther than Saqqara and Dahshûr, nor out into the
desert beyond the river.

The first problem Greaves discussed in the *Pyramidographia* was the old question of why the Egyptians had
erected the pyramids. Many contemporary writers believed
them to be granaries that the Egyptians had forced the
captive Hebrews to build, but this explanation could not
be correct, Greaves was certain. The biblical account of the
Israelites in Egypt specifically states that the Hebrews had
constructed the granaries out of brick only. Therefore, the
pyramids, most of which were built of heavy stone blocks,
could not be the structures described in the Bible. Furthermore, all the best classical authors and the Arab writers
described pyramids as tombs. Ancient Arabic works relate
how a medieval caliph forced his way into the Pyramid of
Cheops, finding there the mummy of a king wearing gold
and precious stones. This discovery clearly indicated that
the pyramid was a tomb (actually the mummy could not
have been that of Cheops because it had been plundered
and destroyed before the end of the Dynastic Period).

Greaves further attacked the idea that the pyramids were
built to be granaries, basing his conclusions on evidence
furnished by mathematical reasoning and by his own explorations. A pyramid-shaped structure makes a poor
granary, since it does not contain as much space as do structures of other shapes. Greaves's explorations of the Great
Pyramid had convinced him that the bulk of it consisted of
solid stone and, therefore, that it could not have been a

storage bin for grain. As for the reason why the Egyptian kings should have wanted to preserve their bodies after death, Greaves suggested that they believed in the transmigration of souls and were afraid that if the body decayed the soul would flee from it.

In the *Pyramidographia*, Greaves gave detailed accounts of the mummies he had seen in Egypt. As Sandys had done, Greaves had purchased some of the statuettes of Egyptian gods that had been found within mummies. The Egyptians had fashioned these statuettes out of stone and metal or had cast them from clay. The mummies had been placed in coffins shaped like human bodies and containing hieroglyph-covered scrolls. A face was sculptured upon each coffin, and each embalmed body, wrapped in cloth, had a mask strapped to it. Despite the passage of many centuries, the mummy cloth had remained in very good condition. Greaves opened a mummy's skull so that he could examine the materials that the ancient Egyptians had used in embalming the body. His examination of the mummy convinced him that Herodotus' account of the embalming process was essentially correct.

Greaves's *Pyramidographia* was the most detailed and sensible account of the Egyptian remains published in the seventeenth century. Greaves did, however, go astray when he discussed the nature of hieroglyphs and tried to sketch the history of Egypt. Like all the other Renaissance scholars, he considered the hieroglyphs to be symbols "expressing the abstractest notions of the minde, by visible similitudes of birds, and beasts, or by representations of some other familiar objects." Forced to depend on the same biblical and classical sources as Ralegh had used, he produced a narrative of Egypt's ancient history no more valid than Ralegh's.

Yet it is clear that Egyptology and Egyptian archaeology were foreshadowed during the sixteenth and seventeenth centuries and that Englishmen played a significant part in what were to evolve into scientific disciplines. As late as 1585 there was no work by an Englishman that described the magnificent ruins of the Nile Valley, but immediately thereafter English commercial agents and travelers began to publish accounts of the ruins that they had seen in Egypt. Their pamphlets and books supplied valuable information which, together with that published by Italian, French, and German travelers, served to correct many of the errors of classical and medieval authors. In the first half of the seventeenth century Sandys and Greaves published the first detailed accounts in English of the Egyptian remains and the first accurate drawings and diagrams of the pyramids. Indeed, John Greaves's *Pyramidographia* remained the most scientifically accurate account of the pyramids until the nineteenth century, when explorers took new measurements of the structures. Nevertheless, much work remained for explorers to do before a complete account of all the ruins in the Nile Valley could be compiled. At the end of the seventeenth century no other writer had traveled as far as Leo Africanus did early in the sixteenth century, and his descriptions of the ruins in Upper Egypt would not satisfy anyone desiring detailed information. Thus the task of making known the antiquities of Upper Egypt fell to the explorers and travelers of the eighteenth century.

# III

# Travelers in Egypt
# During
# the Eighteenth Century

AKING up where the Renaissance travelers had left off, eighteenth-century explorers succeeded in examining and sketching ruins of the Nile Valley from Alexandria to the land of the ancient Cushite kingdoms in upper Nubia, including the great temples of the south. Like the earlier travelers, they collected and brought home many smaller antiquities of Egypt. They were the first explorers to make accurate copies of hieroglyphic inscriptions. The life of the Egyptians as pictured in the frescoes and paintings on the walls of their temples and tombs was beginning to interest explorers, and they began excavating the hidden remains of ancient Egypt and cleaning out the temples and tombs. By 1798, when the French landed in Egypt with their soldiers and savants, the way had already been prepared for the great outburst of archaeological activity that took place in Egypt during the early years of the nineteenth century.

During the late seventeenth century and the first half of the eighteenth, the increasing interest in the ancient civilization along the Nile brought to Egypt a number of travelers about whom, unfortunately, little is known today.[1] Sometime between 1660 and 1677 a Scotsman named Melton visited Giza. He was the first British traveler to examine carefully the large rectangular structures, now called mastabas, near the Pyramids, and he guessed correctly that these structures might have served as the tombs of Egyptian nobles. Unfortunately, Melton's explorations and conclusions remained unknown in England.

At the end of the seventeenth century a scholarly traveler, Ellis Veryard, visited Giza. Veryard gave a description of the Pyramids of Giza in an account of his travels that he published in 1707, but his researches added nothing to what the earlier travelers had already revealed about the Pyramids.

In the years 1705 to 1707, John Perceval, the first earl of Egmont and a Fellow of the Royal Society, traveled in Egypt. His researches, like Veryard's, contributed little to what was already known about the antiquities of Alexandria, Cairo, and Giza.

Paul Spencer, a student of Irish antiquities, visited Egypt in 1721. Spencer made drawings of pyramids, obelisks, and other ruins, but none of the drawings have survived.

In 1750, Robert Wood, who later published the first important description of ancient Baalbek in Lebanon, visited Giza and toured the chambers of the Great Pyramid. He failed to make any original discoveries at Giza, however. In short, while the work of these travelers stimulated interest in the Egyptian ruins, they contributed little that was new to Englishmen's knowledge of Egypt.

A slightly more important figure in the history of Egyptology was Robert Huntington, who made two visits to Egypt between 1670 and 1681. An orientalist, Huntington collected Coptic manuscripts and hieroglyphic inscriptions. He was the first of many scholars to suggest that the hieroglyphs were ideograms, each hieroglyph representing an entire word or idea rather than a letter or sound. The reverse was true, but Huntington did perform a useful service in insisting on the necessity of securing accurate copies of hieroglyphic inscriptions before attempting to decipher them.

Of all the travelers who visited Egypt in the eighteenth century, none possessed a higher reputation for courage and for scientific ability than did Thomas Shaw, who explored the ruins at Alexandria and Giza sometime during the years 1720 to 1733. Although a learned student of Greek and Arabic and a naturalist of some importance, Shaw accomplished little in his Egyptian inquiries. He did observe that the ancient Egyptians had cut each obelisk out of a quarry as one huge block, an important fact that earlier travelers had not noticed. On the top of the Sphinx's head at Giza, Shaw found a hole that he believed might lead to a tunnel connecting the Sphinx with the well in the Great Pyramid. Actually the original sculptors had dug out the hole merely to hold the "tongue" of an attached crown, which had disappeared centuries before Shaw's visit. The pyramids, according to Shaw, could not have been tombs but had been, instead, temples. The great stone vessel in the King's Chamber of the Great Pyramid was not a sarcophagus at all but merely a chest in which the priests had placed religious instruments. Bizarre as his conception of the function of the pyramid appears today, it was no less reasonable an interpretation than any other in the light of contemporary evidence.[2]

To modern-day historians, John Montagu, the fourth earl of Sandwich, is primarily remembered as first lord of the admiralty during the American Revolutionary War. Yet he has a legitimate claim to a place in the history books for his activities during an Egyptian tour he made in 1737. One of the first sites he visited was that of Heliopolis (On), a city the ancient Egyptians held sacred to the Sun God. Only a tall obelisk and a great mound, similar to many other mounds in the delta, marked the city's location. Sandwich realized that these mounds hid the remains of ancient cities, but no attempt to clear the earth from the remains was to be made during the eighteenth century. At Giza, Sandwich noticed the smaller pyramids clustered around the three larger ones. Originally each of the larger pyramids had had two smaller pyramids near it: an empty one for funerary rites and one which had served as a tomb for the wife or mother of the Pharaoh buried in the large pyramid. Sandwich remarked on their existence but could not explain their purpose. The pyramids at Saqqara and at Dahshûr held his close attention for many days. His book contains the first accurate description of the Step Pyramid at Saqqara, built by King Zoser (Djoser), of the Third Dynasty. In creating this structure, the Egyptians had progressed from the mastaba to the first true pyramid. Sandwich described the physical appearance of the two large stone pyramids—one of which is called the Bent, or Blunted, Pyramid because of a slumped appearance at the top—erected at Saqqara by Snefru (Snofru), the father of Cheops and the first king of the Fourth Dynasty. He explored the interior of the northernmost pyramid at Dahshûr and eventually published the first diagram of its passages and chambers. The interior of this pyramid was empty, and only the strange corbeled ceiling lent it some interest. Sandwich examined a large tomb at Giza, and his work was one of the earliest to use the Arabic term mastaba.[3]

The first English traveler to voyage up the Nile farther than the pyramids at Saqqara was Richard Pococke, an Anglican clergyman who visited Egypt in the winter of 1737–38.[4] Pococke viewed the pyramids at Giza, Saqqara, and Dahshûr and later had printed the first picture of the oddly shaped step pyramid at Medûm, built by Snefru. The Medûm Pyramid resembles a tower rising out of a large

27

mound. Its strange shape resulted from its partial dismemberment during the period of the New Kingdom, and the mount consists in part of debris from the original main structure.

From Giza a caravan carried Pococke out into the Faiyûm. There he took notes on the condition of the pyramids, on the site of ancient Arsinoë (Crocodilopolis), and on the ruins of the so-called Labyrinth, a temple erected during the reign of Amenemhet IV, before finally reaching Lake Moeris (Birket Qârûn, or Lake of the Horns).

After returning to Cairo, Pococke gathered supplies for a trip up the Nile. A dahabeah, a kind of sailing vessel used by all travelers who ventured beyond Saqqara and Dahshûr, transported him upriver all the way to the First Cataract at Aswân and even some distance beyond. During the course of this trip Pococke toured ancient sites at El Ashmûnein, Akhmîm, Lycopolis, Dendera, Ombos (Kom Ombos), Deir el-Bahri, Abydos, Qift (Coptos), Thebes, Erment (Armant, the site of ancient Hermonthis), Isna (Esna), Idfou (Edfu), Gobel Silsileh (Mountain of the Chain), the islands of Elphantine and Philae, and the ruins of Syene at Aswân. Pococke published the first drawings and detailed descriptions of the great temples of Karnak and Luxor at Thebes; of the huge sitting Colossi of Memnon, the two gigantic statues of Amenemhet III, also at Thebes; and of the magnificent temples at Ombos, Isna, Idfou, and Dendera. In a valley near Thebes the Egyptians had cut out of the cliffs a number of royal tombs. Inside they decorated the walls with paintings and hieroglyphic inscriptions. Pococke published plans of some of these tombs and commented enthusiastically on the beauty of the frescoes.

Pococke had his limitations as an explorer. He was not very much interested in copying hieroglyphic inscriptions, and those copies he did make were inaccurate. Strangely, he failed to describe, among other important objects, one of the most interesting monuments that he visited, the Temple of Hatshepsut at Deir el-Bahri. Nevertheless, in a stay of only slightly longer than two months, he accomplished an amazing amount of significant work. His drawings of the Egyptian ruins revealed the architectural wonders of Upper Egypt to Europe in a dramatic new way and were a major influence stimulating increased interest in the ancient Egyptian ruins.

While Pococke was exploring the Egyptian antiquities, another dahabeah was carrying Frederick Lewis Norden up the Nile.[5] A Dane by birth, Norden spent much of his life in England, and he published both an early volume of his drawings and later his travel narrative there. In Egypt, Norden visited most of the temples and sites Pococke had. He did, however, miss the large temple at Dendera, though he published accounts of temples at Qua el-Kebir and at Medinet Habu that Pococke had neglected. Obelisks fascinated Norden, and his travel narrative contains descriptions of those at Alexandria, Heliopolis, Luxor, and Karnak and on Philae. As Shaw had done, he noted that the Egyptians had cut each obelisk from one great piece of stone.

Reaching Aswân, Norden determined to be the first European to sail beyond Egypt into Nubia, a land of savage Negro tribes and the location of the ancient Kingdom of Cush (Ethiopia). The dahabeah easily cleared the First Cataract and carried him on to the Egyptian and Roman sites at Debot (Bigga), Kalabsha, Dendûr, Gerf Hussein, El Dakkeh, Kubban, Es Sebua, Amada, and El Diwân (El Dirr). Although he had hoped to reach the Second Cataract at Wadi Halfa, the owner of the dahabeah refused to venture farther ínto uncivilized territory, and Norden had to turn back. A short trip south would have brought him to the Temple of Abu Simbel, never seen by a European traveler. Even so, Norden published the first description of any Nubian temples by a European.

The Eighteenth Dynasty temple at Amada was one of the most interesting. The Copts had once used this ancient building as a church, hiding the pagan hieroglyphs with plaster and pictures of Christian saints. But their attempt to conceal the hieroglyphs merely preserved them from harm. Inside the temple excellently preserved hieroglyphs could be seen in those places where the plaster had fallen off.

Charles Perry, a doctor famous for his many medical writings, voyaged up the Nile to Aswân during the years 1739 to 1742. In most respects Perry merely duplicated Pococke's trip, but he did show an interest in certain aspects of ancient Egypt neglected by earlier travelers. In his narrative appears the earliest description of the Isis Temple of Hebit (Behbit el-Hagar) in the delta and the most detailed account of the beautiful frescoes in the tombs of the Beni Hasan necropolis. Inside the Temple of Karnak, the grandest of the Theban remains, Perry viewed the great frescoes of the Battle of Kadesh—painted by order of Ramses II. Perry recommended to future travelers the "neat, elegant, and beautiful" paintings in the tombs of the Valley of the Kings.[6]

This interest in such things as the Kadesh battle scenes and the paintings in the tombs was very significant. Inevitably it would lead to a search for information about ancient Egyptian life and history, not in the misleading classical writings but among the paintings and inscriptions to be found on the Egyptian monuments.

Richard Dalton, an artist and a founder of the Royal Academy of Arts, visited Egypt in 1749. He made drawings of the obelisks at Alexandria, Pompey's Pillar, and the pyramids at Giza and Saqqara. Dalton lacked great skill as an artist, and his illustrations of Egyptian antiquities did not improve on those which Pococke, Norden, and Perry had made available.[7]

One of the first visitors to conduct extensive excavations

around an Egyptian monument was Edward Wortley Montagu, a leading figure of the eighteenth century, a cousin of the fourth earl of Sandwich, and a friend of Pococke. In 1764, Montagu spent several weeks digging around the foundations of Pompey's Pillar. The discoveries he made there led him to believe that the Roman emperor Vespasian had set up the column. Actually a Roman prefect, one Pompeius, had had the column raised in honor of the emperor Diocletian. Montagu's excavations do demonstrate, however, that by the late eighteenth century scholars were becoming increasingly aware of the need to seek new means of securing information about the Egyptian ruins. Montagu published the earliest reproductions of the hieroglyphic inscriptions in the desert between the Nile and Suez and in the Sinai Peninsula.[8]

In the spring of 1777 a boat deposited Eyles Irwin, an employee of the East India Company, ashore at Quseir (Kosseir), a port on the Egyptian coast of the Red Sea. After many difficulties Irwin finally managed to arrange a journey across the desert to Cairo and then down the Nile to Alexandria. In 1780 he returned to the Red Sea by the same route. He eventually published an account of his adventures, in which he described ruins he had seen in Lower Egypt. He added little that earlier travelers had not already reported about these antiquities.[9]

Despite the fact that almost every traveler who had visited Giza during the past two centuries had explored the interior passages and chambers of the Great Pyramid, in the mid-eighteenth century this immense monument still contained many secrets. As mentioned earlier, on entering the pyramid and going up the Ascending Passage to the chambers above, tourists and explorers passed the deep hole in the rock that they usually described as a well. No one had yet attempted to descend the well. Nor, it appears, had anyone been curious about whether the Egyptians had excavated any passages and chambers in the rock below the pyramid.

Above the King's Chamber the Egyptians had built the five relieving chambers described earlier. They had also built air channels into the sides of the Great Pyramid to provide for circulation of the air in its inner passages. With the exception of George Sandys, Renaissance travelers in Egypt had never even suspected the existence of relieving chambers and air passages.

When Edward Wortley Montagu arrived in Egypt, he brought with him Nathaniel Davison, the British consul general at Algiers.[10] During the summer and fall of 1765, Davison made many trips to Giza, where he carried out the most systematic explorations of the pyramids that were undertaken until the early nineteenth century.

Davison made his most important discoveries in the Great Pyramid. Using a rope, a lantern, and a lighted candle and assisted by a crew of superstitious Arabs, Davison managed to lower himself 155 feet into the well. The well, he discovered, consisted of three shafts, the lower two of which were much longer than the upper one. Stones and rubbish completely clogged the lowest shaft and prevented Davison from descending farther. Next Davison directed his attention to the King's Chamber. He found a passage, almost filled with bats' dung, that led into "a long, broad, but low place" just above the King's Chamber. This was the lowest of the relieving chambers. Egyptologists still refer to it as Davison's Chamber. Before leaving Giza, he made copies of the hieroglyphs inscribed in the tombs which the Egyptians had cut into the cliffs of the plateau.

The chief value of Davison's activities at Giza was that they encouraged such later pyramid enthusiasts as Colonel Howard Vyse, John Perring, Charles Piazzi Smyth, John Dixon, and Flinders Petrie to continue the exploration of the Great Pyramid and the search for the secrets of its construction.

In July, 1768, only a short time after Davison left Egypt, James Bruce, the most celebrated African explorer of the eighteenth century, arrived in Alexandria.[11] Bruce intended to follow the Nile to its source in the heart of Africa, and he had spent years mastering Arabic and otherwise preparing himself for this experience. The events of Bruce's journey to the source of the Blue Nile are too well known to require further discussion, but most writers concerned with the history of African exploration have discussed Bruce's trip from the geographical standpoint only and have neglected his significant contributions to Egyptology.

An enlarged version of the dahabeah, which the natives called a *cauja*, carried Bruce up the Nile. During the course of his journey from Alexandria to Aswân, Bruce took notes on the condition of the ruins at Giza, Dahshûr, Meydûm, El Minya, El Ashmûnein, Akhmîm, Qau el-Kebir, Dendera, Luxor, Karnak, Ombos, Isna, Idfou, and Syene, near Aswân.

Bruce was keenly aware of the importance of the hieroglyphic inscriptions at Thebes. There were, he observed, three basic types of hieroglyphs in the Theban inscriptions. These three types he called "hieroglyphics, the Mummy character, and the Ethiopic." Bruce was, of course, referring to the three states in the evolution of the Egyptian alphabet which Egyptologists today call hieroglyphic, hieratic, and demotic.

The temples of Karnak and Luxor impressed him more than any others he had seen in Egypt. On the walls of both temples he found scenes depicting what has since been identified as the Battle of Kadesh. Bruce's description of these paintings indicates that he realized their possible importance for history:

D

Upon the outside of the walls at Carnac and Luxor there seems to be an historical engraving instead of hieroglyphics; this we had not met before. It is a representation of men, horses, chariots, and battles; some of the attitudes are freely and well drawn, they are rudely scratched upon the surface of the stone, as some of the hieroglyphics at Thebes are. The weapons the men make use of are short javelins, such as are common at this day among the inhabitants of Egypt, only they have feathered wings like arrows. There is also distinguished among the rest, the figure of a man on horseback, with a lion fighting furiously by him, and Diodorus says, Osimandyas was so represented at Thebes. This whole composition merits great attention.

In the tombs in the Valley of the Kings the liveliness of the scenes on the walls astonished Bruce. In one tomb the Egyptians had painted the picture of a crocodile seizing an Apis bull, pictures of the scarab beetle and a monster resembling Typhon, and two pictures of an Egyptian playing a harp. Bruce and an assistant went to work making copies of the tomb pictures.

A large red-granite sarcophagus also lay in the tomb. Though Bruce did not know it at the time, he had visited the tomb of Ramses II. He was the first European to publish a description of this tomb, which Egyptologists today call Bruce's Tomb.

From Aswân, Bruce did not press on into Nubia, but later during his travels in Ethiopia he reached the area in the northern Sudan where the ancient Kingdom of Cush had flourished. He was the first English traveler to visit the ruins of Aksum (Axum) and Meroë; indeed, few European travelers had been there. Had Bruce chosen to describe the Cushite ruins in detail, he would have performed a notable service for Egyptology, but he merely referred briefly to the obelisks at Aksum and noted the position of the ancient capital of Meroë. Bruce subscribed to the common, but erroneous, belief that the Ethiopians, whose civilization had been centered on the Isle of Meroë, had taught the Egyptians the arts of civilization.

In 1791, James Bruce's account of his explorations of the Blue Nile inspired William George Browne, a young student of Oriental languages at Oxford, to put aside his scholarly studies and travel to Egypt, where he hoped to explore the oases in the eastern region of the Sahara Desert and to journey, if circumstances permitted, to the source of the White Nile.[12]

Browne failed to reach the White Nile, although he did eventually travel to El Fasher, a desert oasis in the Sudan and the capital of the Negro kingdom of Darfur. Before setting out for Darfur, Browne had sailed down the Nile to Aswân. He later published descriptions of the temples and ancient city sites along the riverbanks. At Medûm, Browne carried out limited excavation of the debris around the pyramid. These excavations revealed that the pyramid consisted of stones held together with cement all the way to the ground. The mysterious desert west of the Nile attracted him. Browne was the first Englishman to study the small Egyptian temple at the oasis of Siwa (Ammonium), and he published the first accounts in English of the Pyramid of Amenemhet III at Hawara and that of Senusert II at Lahun. The brick construction of these monuments sets them apart from other pyramids.

Essentially Browne was a scholarly recluse who could not resist the call of distant lands. After many years of quiet, scholarly life in England, he traveled east again to explore Asia Minor. In 1812 a band of nomads killed him in a mountain pass in northern Persia as he was attempting to reach the Moslem khanates of central Asia.

The visitors to Egypt in the eighteenth century—and it must be remembered that there were as many German,

French, and Italian explorers as there were English—made great progress in compiling detailed descriptions of all the ancient structures along the Nile. They achieved success both in describing and mapping those ruins that lay some distance from the Nile in the desert and in exploring the Egyptian remains in the delta on the north and in Nubia and the Sudan on the far south. The French scholars who went to Egypt with Napoleon in 1798 added nothing to what the earlier explorers had already discovered about the physical remains of ancient Egypt. During the eighteenth century serious travelers became interested in making copies of hieroglyphic inscriptions and of the paintings that they found on the sides of obelisks and on the walls of temples and tombs. These efforts at responsible copying actually were very feeble, but at least travelers were demonstrating an awareness of the potential importance of such activities.

There were, of course, many limitations to the work that these early Egyptologists accomplished. In the south, Abu Simbel and the great temples of lower Nubia remained undiscovered. The pyramids of Napata, Nuri, and Meroë awaited systematic exploration. The biblical cities of the delta—Heliopolis, Tanis (Zoan), Bubastis, and Pithom remained unexcavated and undescribed. Archaeologists had yet to discover the ancient Greek trading stations of the delta, and no one suspected the existence of prehistoric remains at Qift and Abydos. Accurate drawings of the hieroglyphs had not yet been made. All these tasks remained for the archaeologists, artists, and travelers of the nineteenth century to perform.

# IV

# Egyptology
## in the Age of Reason

HE upsurge of interest in ancient Egyptian civilization touched many persons besides the learned travelers, with their notebooks in hand, sailing up and down the Nile in the trustworthy dahabeahs. Interest in Egyptian studies spread to educated men who were unable to visit Egypt. These armchair Egyptologists began to assemble collections of Egyptian antiquities and to publish, in the journals of the various antiquarian and scientific societies of England and Europe, articles on Egyptian culture. Historians wrote of the history and civilization of ancient Egypt. The embalming practices of the Egyptians attracted the attention of medical doctors, and students of ancient and Oriental languages studied the hieroglyphs. Interest in Egyptology became so pervasive that it even influenced the architects who designed the houses and gardens of the great lords and ladies of England.

Both public and private collections of Egyptian antiquities were formed. Foreigners who visited England in the eighteenth century took notice of the "abundance of ancient

37

Egyptian monuments" that they saw in museums and private collections.[1]

In 1756, Parliament passed an act establishing the British Museum. When this national museum opened six years later, it contained a collection of Egyptian lamps, papyri, statuettes, and other small objects that had been willed to it by Sir Hans Sloane, one of the founders of the museum, and by Colonel William Lethieullier and Pitt Lethieullier, well-known travelers in Egypt. One of the earliest important private collectors of Egyptian antiquities was Dr. Richard Mead, a famous physician. His collection contained books, manuscripts, statuary, coins, jewelry, drawings, and various small objects from Egypt and other Near Eastern lands. Matthew Duane, a trustee of the British Museum, interested himself in collecting ancient Near Eastern coins, and in the course of his hunt for old coins he acquired a number of Egyptian antiquities as well. Thus in the eighteenth century can be discerned the origin of interest in collecting Egyptian antiquities that became a passion with members of the upper class in the Victorian Age.

The continuing interest in Egyptology led a group of antiquarians to organize the Egyptian Society.[2] On December 11, 1741, the fourth earl of Sandwich presided over a meeting at Lebeck's Head Tavern in Chandos Street, London. Others present who had traveled in Egypt were Richard Pococke, Frederick Lewis Norden, and Charles Perry. William Stukeley, the most famous antiquarian of the eighteenth century, and several of his friends also attended. The men at the meeting agreed to form a society whose purpose would be to promote and preserve "Egyptian and other ancient learning." They elected Sandwich president, under the Oriental title "sheik." The membership consisted of those travelers who had actually visited Egypt and those, known as "philoaegyptians," who merely possessed some interest in Egyptian antiquities. The members planned to hold meetings at two-week intervals during the months from November to April of each year. At a meeting held on January 22, 1742, they added a number of new members to the society. The Egyptian Society failed to survive, however, and was disbanded early in 1743.

Although the Egyptian Society suffered an early death, many of its members also belonged to the Society of Antiquaries of London, which had become a permanent institution in 1717. The members of the Society of Antiquaries maintained an interest in Egyptological subjects throughout the eighteenth and nineteenth centuries. In 1770 the society published its first edition of *Archaeologia*, which became an annual publication. Many subsequent issues contained articles describing Egyptian remains or aspects of ancient Egyptian civilization.

The great interest in ancient Egypt also revealed itself in renewed attempts to work out a reliable account of the history of that ancient land.[3] A number of scholars attempted to unravel the confused chronology of ancient Egypt. Sir Isaac Newton, in his *Chronology of Ancient Kingdoms Amended* (1728), tackled this problem. The most famous eighteenth-century work on the chronology of the Egyptians and other ancient peoples was the *Chronological Antiquities* (1752) of John Jackson, an Anglican theological controversialist. Whereas Newton and Jackson wrote for the scholar specializing in ancient history, a French writer, Charles Rollin, published a popular account of Egyptian civilization in his *Ancient History*, which appeared in an English translation in 1829 and won great popularity with the English-reading public.

Universal histories, works of the sort that are today called world histories, were as popular in the eighteenth century as they are in modern times. Two of the most widely read of the universal histories, both containing accounts of Egyptian history were *A General History of the World* (1764–

67), by William Guthrie, and *Universal History, Ancient and Modern* (1802), by William Mavor.

The authors of these histories—both the ones for scholars and those for general readers—relied basically on the same works for their factual material. The lists of pharaohs of Manetho and of Eratosthenes, classical descriptions of Egypt, and the Bible constituted the main sources. Newton, Jackson, Rollin, and the other historians of the eighteenth century accepted uncritically the factual information contained in these sources; thus their discussions of Egyptian history demonstrated no improvement over what the reader could find in Ralegh's *History of the World*.

The historians of the eighteenth century did, however, achieve one important innovation. They based their descriptions of the ruins along the Nile as much on those of modern travelers as on those of classical authors. When, for example, Jackson described the Pyramids of Giza, he gave the measurements of their heights and other dimensions that he had found in the *Pyramidographia* of John Greaves. Descriptions of the Labyrinth and the obelisks and temples at Thebes came from Richard Pococke's *Description of the East*. This use of modern sources marked a step forward in the long struggle to free Egyptology from the errors in the classical writings.

In the eighteenth century all accounts of ancient Egypt and its civilization, with three exceptions, were either parts of universal histories or of histories of the entire Mediterranean area. Only three scholars wrote separate dissertations on ancient Egypt. Thomas Greenhill's *Nepoxmoeia: Or the Art of Embalming* (1705) was the earliest such treatise; it will be discussed later in this chapter, in the section on accounts of mummification. In 1786, Michael Lord, a professor of Greek at Cambridge, edited and published a treatise by John Woodward on the merits of Egyptian culture, and a Scottish antiquarian, Alexander Gordon, attempted to write a history of Egypt.[4]

The contention of most historians that the Hebrews had not acquired civilized manners before their sojourn in Egypt, the cradle of Western culture, disturbed Woodward, a geologist famous for his defense of catastrophism. In an attempt to disprove this belief, Woodward tried to show that the ancient Egyptians themselves really lacked any degree of culture. His treatise, "Of the Wisdom of the Antient Egyptians," consisted of a long and fruitless polemic against the ancient Egyptians.

The major problem faced by any eighteenth-century scholar who attempted to write a treatise on Egyptian civilization was, of course, the fact that no one knew how to read the hieroglyphs. Hence, they had no way of consulting Egyptian inscriptions and other native sources for information. Indeed, many scholars believed that the hieroglyphs would always remain untranslatable, and others thought that even if they could read them they would gain no really valuable information about the civilization of Egypt, since the hieroglyphs were, they believed, only symbols that expressed mystical concepts.

Alexander Gordon became interested in this problem during the late 1730's. Gordon possessed an excellent knowledge of Latin and Greek, and he had also studied the prehistoric remains of Great Britain. In 1737 he published two treatises on hieroglyphic inscriptions. In these works he attempted to decipher the meaning of the hieroglyphs found on mummies. His efforts proved unsuccessful; they failed to produce any worthwhile methods of approach that future investigators could make use of.

In 1741, Gordon finished work on a manuscript entitled "An Essay Towards Illustrating the History, Chronology, and Mythology, of the Antient Egyptians." The manuscript, which was never published owing to Gordon's untimely death, would have been the first book-length work in English concerned entirely with the history of Egypt.

In the same year in which Alexander Gordon published his two volumes on the Egyptian hieroglyphs, Bishop William Warburton published *The Divine Legation of Moses* in which he attacked the hieroglyphic theories of Athanasius Kircher and presented the first really useful discussion of hieroglyphic writing.[5] Warburton denied that the hieroglyphs were mystical symbols that the Egyptian priests had used to conceal their religious dogmas. He insisted that the Egyptians had developed the hieroglyphic system of writing as a practical device for recording their laws, noting historical events, and keeping accounts of daily business transactions. At the beginning of its evolution, Warburton explained, the hieroglyphic script had consisted of pictographs but had gradually evolved into a true alphabet. Noting that more than one kind of hieroglyphic writing existed, he suggested that through daily use a simpler version of hieroglyphic script had emerged which the Egyptians found much easier to write. Warburton thus perceived the basis for the development of the hieratic and demotic scripts from the hieroglyphic. All these statements were brilliant innovations and greatly advanced hieroglyphic studies.

Warburton's speculations concerning the hieroglyphic script did not, however, appear first in his *Divine Legation of Moses*. Another scholar and writer on theological subjects, Henry Coventry, adopted Warburton's ideas and published them in his *Philemon to Hydaspes*, a dialogue concerned with the nature of ancient religion. Warburton subsequently accused Coventry of plagiarism, a somewhat unfair charge since Coventry had acknowledged his debt to Warburton.

Coventry and Warburton did not entirely rule out the function of the hieroglyphs as sacred symbols. Both maintained—although Coventry stressed this point much more than Warburton—that after the development of a cursive system of writing the Egyptians had restricted the use of hieroglyphic script to the expression of religious concepts and ideas. They were, of course, wrong on this point. The Egyptians continued to use the hieroglyphs to record historical events, for example, long after the development of the hieratic and demotic scripts.

Warburton's speculations about hieroglyphic writing attracted considerable attention, but few writers adopted his ideas. Richard Pococke, in an appendix to his *A Description of the East*, demonstrated a knowledge of Warburton's analysis, but he did not agree with it. Richard Clayton, the bishop of Clogher and a member of the Society of Antiquaries, though impressed by Warburton's ideas about hieroglyphic writing, did not use them in a treatise he published on hieroglyphs and pagan mythology. Nevertheless, Warburton was such an important contemporary theologian that his ideas could not be ignored, and with the passage of time his concept of hieroglyphic writing gained adherents.

In the eighteenth century researchers who attempted to investigate hieroglyphic writing were often led astray by a tendency to identify the hieroglyphs, in nature if not also in form, with the ideograms of the Chinese writing system. These views received formal shape in 1761, when John Turberville Needham, a well-known scientist, published in Latin a *Dissertation Concerning the Egyptian Inscription Found at Turin*. In this work he argued that the Egyptians had founded China as a colony and that there existed an intimate relationship between the Chinese ideograms and the Egyptian hieroglyphs. If Needham had been right in his conclusions, scholars, by comparative studies of the Chinese writing and that of the Egyptians, could have soon deciphered the hieroglyphic inscriptions.

Opposition to Needham's theories soon arose both on the

Continent and in England. He had based his conclusions on a study of an alleged Egyptian inscription on a "bust of Isis" in the Turin museum. Edward Wortley Montagu believed this bust to be of modern origin, and through his persistence Johann Joachim Winckelmann, the greatest contemporary authority on ancient art, was persuaded to examine the bust. Winckelmann pronounced it a recent forgery.

The Royal Society took an official interest in the controversy over the Turin bust. The leaders of the society sent an appeal to the Jesuits stationed in Peking. The Jesuits were the only European scholars of the time who had an intimate knowledge of Chinese. The society asked the Jesuits to decide whether the markings on the bust resembled Chinese ideograms and to comment on the possibility that there had been an Egyptian influence on China. The Jesuits replied that the symbols on the bust were not Chinese characters, and that they knew of no evidence that would support the idea that there had been an Egyptian influence on China.

So much opposition from respectable scholars should have put an end to the controversy. But it persisted into the nineteenth and even the twentieth centuries. Respectable scholars did, however, cease to consider the theory seriously after Champollion began to decipher the hieroglyphs.

The Egyptian mummies also began to attract serious scientific attention in the eighteenth century. For the first time medical doctors began actually dissecting mummies to study the Egyptian process of embalming and identify the embalming materials.

In 1705, Thomas Greenhill, a London doctor and the author of various scientific papers on surgical experiments, published his *Nepoxnoeia*, the first important treatise on ancient Egyptian civilization, and particularly on the Egyptian methods of mummification.[6] Greenhill's account of Egyptian civilization did not improve on the narratives of

Ralegh, Newton, Jackson, or Rollin, and he based his discussion of Egyptian embalming practices on information taken from Herodotus and Diodorus. Like the two ancient writers, Greenhill thought the Egyptians had believed in the transmigration of souls and had preserved the human body so that at some future time the soul could return to it.

Pictures of mummies in various stages of being unwrapped illustrated his work. Greenhill had never himself unrolled a mummy, but he had viewed a number of mummies in private collections, and, using a corpse, had tried to extract a brain through the nostrils as Herodotus had described the ancient Egyptians doing. Greenhill concluded that it could not be done, but the fault lay with Greenhill's methods, not with the basic process.

Despite its serious shortcomings Greenhill's *Nepoxnoeia* remained the best compilation of material on this subject until the publication of Thomas Joseph Pettigrew's *History of Egyptian Mummies* in 1834.

It had become clear that if Egyptologists were ever going to acquire any more knowledge of the embalming process than they could find in the classics skilled surgeons would have to undertake dissections of mummies. The first person to conduct such a dissection was a Dr. Middleton, who unwrapped and dissected a mummy at Cambridge. Dr. John Hadley published the first account of the surgical examination of a mummy. Hadley dissected the mummy on December 16, 1763, in his London home. A large number of surgeons and interested spectators attended (similar large crowds became an integral part of mummy dissections during succeeding years). While Hadley's efforts proved highly entertaining to the onlookers, the pitch that the Egyptians had used in embalming the mummy had so badly damaged its tissues that he learned little from the dissection.

After Hadley, only one other person carried out the scientific dissection of a mummy in this period. A German professor, John Frederick Blumenbach, dissected a number of mummies in England in 1792. Blumenbach had earlier performed surgical examinations of mummies on the Continent. Blumenbach cut open a number of mummies—both human and animal—which he secured from the British Museum and from various private collections in London. Unfortunately, he lacked the necessary skills to conduct truly scientific investigations, and his researches produced even less information about the embalming process than had Hadley's. Blumenbach did, however, realize that the methods of mummification had undergone changes during the course of Egyptian history and that mummies could be placed in categories according to the periods in which they had been mummified. This discovery became useful only after the hieroglyphs had been deciphered and an Egyptian time scale had been worked out.

Over the centuries Egyptology has attracted a large number of eccentrics and disciples of bizarre theories. Among them have been the pyramid cultists, whom scientists have dubbed "pyramidiots," and the cultural diffusionists.[7] The pyramidiots claimed to have uncovered secret information about the past, present, and future locked in the measurements of the Egyptian pyramids. The cultural diffusionists believed either that every ancient civilization originated with an Egyptian colony or that wandering Egyptians greatly influenced all the other ancient nations. Pyramidiocy and cultural diffusionism often go together. Thus the anonymous author of *The Origin and Antiquity of Our English Weights and Measures Discovered by Their Near Agreement with Such Standards That Are Now Found in One of the Egyptian Pyramids*, published in 1706, maintained that from his study of the pyramids' measurements he had discovered the English metrological system to have derived from that of the Egyptians.

Two cultural diffusionists of the late eighteenth century

were Frederick Samuel Schmidt and Charles Vallancy. In 1779, Schmidt published an article in *Archaeologia: Or Miscellaneous Tracts, Relating to Antiquity*, in which he sought to prove that the classical civilization of Greece began with the establishment of a number of Egyptian colonies there. Vallancy, a member of the Society of Antiquaries of Ireland, published a number of works in which he insisted that the ancient Egyptian, Persian, and Hindustani languages had influenced the development of Celtic language. Both Schmidt and Vallancy claimed knowledge of ancient Egypt that in a time before the deciphering of hieroglyphics they could not possibly possess.

As in other periods, Egyptology made some impact during the eighteenth century on the popular culture of England.[8] A widely enjoyed novel of the day—a mammoth eight-volume work—was Thomas Lediard's translation of *Sethos*, by Jean Terrasson. Terrasson had based his fictional work on the classical tales connected with the life and exploits of Sesostris (Senusert III of the Middle Kingdom).

Lediard, a major historian of the period, also translated from the German an architectural treatise, *Plan of Civil and Historical Architecture*, by Johann Fischer von Erlach, containing much material (unfortunately including many erroneous details), on Egyptian buildings. As knowledge of Egyptian monuments increased, English architects began to place reproductions of obelisks, pyramids, and hieroglyphic inscriptions in the great mansions and formal gardens of England. Among many examples of eighteenth-century houses bearing Egyptian ornamentation are Stowe, Chiswick Park, Holkham Hall, Castle Howard, and South Lodge.

The scholars who engaged in studies of Egypt during the eighteenth century may appear, in retrospect, to have pursued a fruitless quest. Their attempts to write Egyptian history were based on sources whose reliability they had no way of determining. The great Sir Isaac Newton failed to work out a reliable chronology for Egyptian history primarily because he did not realize the limitations of the sources he was using in his calculations. The Neoplatonic theories concerning the hieroglyphs, which Athanasius Kircher had propagated, still held the scholarly world in their grip. An even more misleading theory, the concept of an essential identity between the Chinese ideograms and the hieroglyphs, had arisen to plague scholars, and the first pyramidiots and cultural diffusionists had appeared to cloud the picture further. Egyptologists learned very little about Egyptian embalming practices from the primitive dissections of mummies performed by eighteenth-century surgeons.

Despite the apparent fruitlessness of all these activities, they did possess great significance. Scholars investigated Egyptian questions during the eighteenth century with a zeal not displayed before. By the end of the century Egyptology was rapidly attaining the popularity that it gained in full measure during the course of the nineteenth century. While the inability to decipher the hieroglyphics kept scholars from writing accurate Egyptian history, the first steps toward eliminating this difficulty were being made. Warburton's ideas helped give some degree of sanity to hieroglyphic studies, and the copying of hieroglyphs made slow but noticeable progress toward a usable degree of accuracy. Most significant of all, of course, was the work of the travelers who brought back to England with them detailed accounts of the remains that the ancient Egyptians had left behind along the banks of the Nile. When the French landed in Egypt in 1798, Europe was ready to receive the news of the discovery of the bilingual inscription on the Rosetta Stone and to follow it up with a new surge of exploratory activity in Egypt. In Egyptology, as in most things, the new age was a natural outgrowth of the old.

# V

# The Dawning
of the Great Age:
British Soldiers
and Explorers in Egypt

ANY historians have dated the beginning of modern Egyptology from Napoleon Bonaparte's invasion of Egypt in 1798.[1] Napoleon brought with him not only soldiers but also many scholars and scientists who made a comprehensive inquiry into the past and present state of Egypt. The results of their efforts appeared in the *Description of Egypt*, a nineteen-volume work published by the French government, and the success of this great survey encouraged the French to support the publication of the Egyptian inscriptions found in temples and upon the papyri. The most significant event of Napoleon's expedition, however, was the uncovering of the Rosetta Stone, a piece of black basalt bearing a bilingual inscription in hieroglyphics, demotic characters, and Greek. The discovery was ultimately to make possible the deciphering of hieroglyphic writing. But, although the French unearthed the Rosetta Stone, they could not keep it. The British army, which invaded Egypt in 1801, eventually claimed the stone and the other artifacts collected by the French savants as prizes of battle.

The British force carried with it a number of individuals who had great interest in Egyptology. One of these, Edward Daniel Clarke, a civilian, later published a massive travel narrative containing not only descriptions of Egyptian antiquities but also an account of the British army in Egypt. Clarke entered Alexandria with the advance guard of British troops because he intended to make certain that the French did not send any Egyptian antiquities back to France. Another British civilian who entered Egypt with similar intentions was William Richard Hamilton, an agent for Lord Elgin. Elgin, the British ambassador to Constantinople, occupied himself with packing Greek statues off from Athens, and he sent Hamilton to Alexandria with orders to seize the French collection of Egyptian remains. Working together, Clarke and Hamilton succeeded in stealing from the French a great many antiquities—including a great green sarcophagus hidden by the French in a hospital ship —that the French had stolen from the Egyptians.

This sarcophagus later involved Clarke in trouble with his fellow scholars. He claimed that it was the tomb of Alexander the Great and wrote a learned dissertation attempting to prove his contention. Of course, since Clarke could not translate the hieroglyphs on the side of the coffin, he had no certain way of proving whose coffin it really was. Clarke held many erroneous beliefs about the Egyptian monuments. A cultural diffusionist, he believed that certain scenes painted on the walls of Egyptian buildings proved that the Egyptians had civilized China and India; and the Great Pyramid at Giza, he was certain, had served as the tomb of Joseph, the leader of the Israelites in Egypt.

Clarke did, however, immediately realize the importance of the inscription on the Rosetta Stone. He knew that through a comparison of the Greek and the hieroglyphic and demotic writings the Egyptian inscription, and hence eventually the hieroglyphic alphabet, could be deciphered.

Luckily for Clarke, a young colonel in the army, Thomas Hilgrove Turner, also had great enthusiasm for Egyptian studies. The Rosetta Stone lay in the house of the French general in Alexandria, however, and the general refused to give it up. Finally Turner collected a detachment of soldiers and seized it. He accompanied the stone all the way to England to make certain that it arrived safely.

In London, Turner gave the stone into the safekeeping of the Society of Antiquaries. The society kept it long enough to make casts of it, which were distributed to the British universities. The society also published translations of the Greek inscription. Accurate translations were a necessity if British scholars were to decipher the Egyptian inscriptions by the comparative method.

The Rosetta Stone, like all the other captured artifacts, finally came to rest in the British Museum. The need to house this and the many other vast acquisitions of Egyptian remains forced a reluctant Parliament to approve major additions to the museum.

The discovery of the Rosetta Stone and the publication of hieroglyphic inscriptions by the French provided powerful stimuli for decipherment of the hieroglyphs.[2] However, the earliest of the nineteenth-century attempts to translate hieroglyphic inscriptions were as fruitless as earlier efforts had been.

Robert Deverell, a graduate of the University of Cambridge and a tutor to the sons of aristocrats, published two works in 1805 and 1816 in which he claimed that he had solved the problem of hieroglyphic translation and proceeded to give an account of what he had learned about ancient Egyptian civilization.

Deverell was both a cultural diffusionist and a pyramidiot. He insisted that ancient Egypt had acquired its civilization from England, whose colony Egypt had been in ancient times. The Egyptians had erected their huge monuments in a pyramidal form because they were trying to build them in the geographical shape of England, which is roughly triangular. The Great Pyramid, for example, was a monument to "England itself." Later the Egyptians had, in turn, established colonies in South America, Japan, and India. No respectable scholar accepted Deverell's ideas.

Two other English scholars who interested themselves in the possibility of translating hieroglyphs, particularly those on the Rosetta Stone, were James Bailey, a classical scholar, and Lord Elgin's assistant, William Richard Hamilton. In 1808, Hamilton read a paper before the Society of Antiquaries on the possibility of deciphering the hieroglyphic inscription on the Rosetta Stone by comparing it with the Greek inscription, and, in 1816, Bailey published a book that suggested the same approach. Neither Hamilton nor Bailey, however, achieved any success in deciphering the hieroglyphic script.

Silvestre de Sacy, a French orientalist, and Johann David Akerblad, a Swedish diplomat and orientalist, carried out the first fruitful studies of the Egyptian texts on the Rosetta Stone. Both of these men had studied Coptic, and both chose to work on the demotic rather than the hieroglyphic text.

De Sacy succeeded in locating the groups of letters in demotic that spelled Ptolemy, Alexander, and Alexandria. But he could not break these names down into separate letters, and his limited alphabet of fifteen demotic letters proved later to be generally incorrect.

Akerblad made much greater progress in deriving a demotic alphabet. He identified the groups of letters that spelled the proper names Arsinoë, Berenice, and Aetos and confirmed the discoveries of de Sacy in regard to the other proper names. Eventually Akerblad produced a demotic alphabet of some twenty-nine letters, of which about half were correct, and he proved as well that the demotic was essentially an alphabetic script. Unfortunately, his belief in the essentially symbolic nature of the hieroglyphs prevented him from attempting to decipher the hieroglyphic text.

De Sacy and Akerblad attained very limited results from their labors. They did not succeed in deriving a complete demotic alphabet, and they also failed to attempt an examination of the hieroglyphic inscription on the Rosetta Stone. Both men published the results of their studies in 1802. It was more than a full decade later before Thomas Young, an English scholar, made the next significant contributions to the study of ancient Egyptian writing.

Young had already established an international reputation as a physicist when he first began his work on the Egyptian alphabets.[3] Young was a brilliant linguist with a knowledge of seven languages. He soon mastered another, Coptic, in hopes it would aid him in his researches into the demotic and hieroglyphic scripts. De Sacy's and Akerblad's work proved a great aid to his inquiries. Concentrating first on the demotic text of the stone, he translated all the words and derived some more of the letters in the demotic alphabet.

In the year 1815–16, Young made a great discovery. Aided by a suggestion from William John Bankes, an English gentleman who owned an obelisk upon which the Egyptians had carved an inscription in both Greek and hieroglyphs, Young came to believe that the Egyptians might have used the hieroglyphs as letters rather than symbols in inscribing the name of a foreign conqueror or king on one of their monuments. In this case only, the Egyptians would have used those hieroglyphs having the appropriate phonetic value as letters without any regard to their regular use as symbols. Young concluded that the ovals, or cartouches, in the hieroglyphic inscription on the Rosetta Stone probably contained the names of these foreign rulers. By a comparison of the hieroglyphic inscription with the Greek text

Young identified the names of Ptolemy and of Berenice, his queen.

Young then proceeded to derive a few of the elements of a hieroglyphic alphabet, although most of his hieroglyphic letters later proved incorrect. In addition, he discovered many of the basic rules about hieroglyphic writing—such as the fact that one must read a hieroglyphic inscription in the direction in which the hieroglyphs face—and he clearly perceived the process by which the hieratic and demotic scripts had developed out of the hieroglyphic writing.

Young published the results of his work in the article on Egypt that he wrote for the 1819 edition of *Encyclopaedia Britannica*. The article reveals the limitations of Young's work that have led scholars to award to Jean François Champollion, the French linguist, the title of first decipherer of the hieroglyphs. Young refused to admit that all the hieroglyphs possessed phonetic values. He believed that the Egyptians had used the hieroglyphs as letters only when writing proper names. Furthermore, his translation of hieroglyphic, and even of demotic, words and phrases was mechanical and hence misleading when the meaning of a group of signs was not perfectly clear. Still, Young had made great advances in the study of the Egyptian writing, and his work proved very helpful to Champollion during the latter's successful efforts to derive a complete system for translating hieroglyphs.

Young soon abandoned the study of hieroglyphic writing, instead devoting his last years to developing a more extended demotic vocabulary and promoting the publication of hieroglyphic inscriptions. In 1819 he formed a group called the Syro-Egyptian Society. The purpose of this society, which consisted mainly of a group of subscribers, was to secure the publication of all the known hieroglyphic inscriptions and to send explorers to copy inscriptions that had been omitted from earlier collections. Lack of money brought the Syro-Egyptian Society to an end after the issuance of only one volume. The Royal Society of Literature agreed to finance the publication of additional volumes, but the third volume, published in 1829, proved to be the last. Young's final work, a demotic dictionary, appeared posthumously.

Like any new development, the phonetic system of hieroglyphic translation excited opposition.[4] In 1826, Gustave Seyffarth, a German Egyptologist, published a work in which he attacked the ideas of Champollion. Seyffarth had devised his own system of hieroglyphic decipherment (which no one but Seyffarth and his followers ever managed to comprehend), and he insisted that the hieroglyphs were nonphonetic signs. Like many bizarre and fundamentally unsound ideas, Seyffarth's theories died a quick death once the initial excitement about them had subsided.

In England there arose another group of critics. In 1829, William Mure, a classical scholar, published an attack on Champollion's theories, which he declared to be both erroneous and impious. Another critic who was troubled about the supposed impiety of Champollion's ideas was Charles William Wall, a professor of Hebrew in the University of Dublin. In 1835, Wall published a book denouncing Warburton, Young, and Champollion as infidels who had put forward ideas that were at variance with Holy Scripture. He also defended the older concept of the hieroglyphs as "sacred symbols." The leading scholarly journals of England —particularly the big three, the *Quarterly Review*, the *Westminster Review*, and the *Edinburgh Review*—considered Seyffarth, Mure, Wall, and other such critics merely cranks.

Several decades passed before hieroglyphic studies revealed any significant information about the history and literature of Egypt. This slow development proved very disappointing to many scholars, and, in 1862 in a book on ancient astronomy, a widely respected intellectual, Sir

George Cornewall Lewis, stated that neither Champollion nor anyone else had succeeded in making accurate hieroglyphic translations. He expressed doubts that hieroglyphic studies would ever produce results useful to the historian. Ironically, Lewis published his book at a time when hieroglyphic studies were becoming much more productive, and subsequent accomplishments in the field made his pronouncements appear foolish.

The Napoleonic Wars encouraged English tourists to visit the East, and during these years a steady flow of tourists went to Egypt. Most travelers chose to hire a dahabeah and sail up the Nile to Aswân, and a number went beyond Aswân into the wilds of Nubia. After the collapse of the Napoleonic Empire, this traffic did not cease but rather grew steadily. Many travelers published narratives of their explorations in Egypt, and most of these books sold well. Much of the literature was of poor quality, but a few travelers did perform useful work by describing many ruins that eighteenth-century explorers had not visited.[5]

The earliest of these explorers were Thomas Legh, M. P., and the Reverend Charles Smelt, who traveled together up the Nile in the winter of 1812–13. Legh later described the many temples, "hewn out of the living rock" of the desert, which he had visited in Nubia. Because of their crude construction he mistakenly concluded that they were far older than those in Egypt. Once again, the inability to read the hieroglyphic inscriptions on the walls of Egyptian monuments had prevented an otherwise competent observer from making an accurate assessment of them.

After the journey of Legh and Smelt a horde of English travelers—artists, adventurers, and explorers—descended on Egypt. James Silk Buckingham, a sea captain and adventurer, who was later to found the periodical *Athanaeum*, explored the area around Aswân in 1813–14. Another traveler, Captain Henry Light, explored the temples in Nubia in May, 1814. In the years 1816 to 1818, the earl of Belmore and a large group of friends went up the Nile as far as Wadi Halfa and the Second Cataract. Beginning in 1819, a Scottish traveler, Sir Archibald Edmonstone, carried out explorations of the ruins in the oases east of the Nile.

In the fall and winter of 1820–21, George Waddington, Fellow of Trinity College, Cambridge, and the Reverend Barnard Hanbury visited the area in the northern Sudan where the ancient Cushite civilization had flourished. They toured the Egyptian ruins on Argo (Arko) Island, the temples at Soleb Sesebi, and the temples of Gebel Barkal (the site of ancient Napata). Although Bruce had passed through the region earlier, Waddington's journal, published in 1822, provided somewhat more information about these ruins than could be found in Bruce's account.

Of all these travelers the one destined to make the most spectacular discovery was John Lewis Burckhardt (who adopted the name Sheik Ibrahim ibn Adullah), a native of Switzerland and a Cambridge scholar.[6] He explored Nubia from 1813 to 1817. The African Association, a London society mainly concerned with promoting the geographical exploration of the interior of Africa, financed his journeys. Although Burckhardt was a student of Arab life and not an Egyptologist, he discovered many long-lost Egyptian remains. At the beginning of his explorations in 1813 he came upon the small temple of the wife of Ramses II and the great temple of Ramses II at Abu Simbel. Sand had blocked the entrance to the large temple and almost covered the four colossi guarding its entrance. Of all Burckhardt's discoveries, the temple complex at Abu Simbel gained him the most fame.

Perhaps the most unlikely traveler to explore the ruins of Egypt during the nineteenth century was Benjamin Disraeli, who landed in "the ancient land of Priestcraft and of Pyramids" in March, 1831, and spent about four months visiting the ruins along the Nile.[7] Disraeli's travels contributed nothing to the development of Egyptology, but they did provide him with material for some of the scenes in his novel *Contarini Fleming*.

During the winter of 1836–37, Alexander Lindsay, the future eighth earl of Balcarres, made the usual tour down the Nile and into Nubia. By 1836 hieroglyphic studies had advanced to such a point that when Lindsay saw the great Kadesh battle scenes on the walls of the temple at Abu Simbel he knew, unlike earlier travelers, that the conquering Pharaoh in the pictures was Ramses II.[8]

By the 1840's, Egyptology and general interest in the ancient civilizations of the East had become one of the leading passions of educated Englishmen. At this time there developed a great demand for popular accounts of the ancient ruins of the Middle East. In answer to this demand English publishers began to put on the market very expensive, multivolumed, heavily illustrated works describing the antiquities of the East. Most of these tomes consisted only of lithographed paintings of Eastern scenes with comments on the biblical and historical significance of each view. In 1855, David Roberts, a Scottish painter of outdoor scenes, produced in his six-volume *The Holy Land* one of the most successful works of this kind.[9] In late 1838, Roberts had arrived in Egypt, where he secured a comfortable dahabeah and set off for an extended tour of the Nile ruins between Cairo and Wadi Halfa. By this time so many travelers and explorers had traveled up the Nile into Nubia and back that the trip could no longer be considered either dangerous or novel.

Roberts made paintings of the ruins and scenes that proved most striking to him. A romantic painter, Roberts liked to add color to his pictures. He did, however, have an appreciation of the massiveness and the grandeur of the

Egyptian ruins, and these qualities were reflected in his paintings.

William Brockedon, an English painter and writer, wrote the descriptions for each of the plates in *The Holy Land*. He attempted to give an account of individual ruins in the light of what Egyptologists had discovered about them, and he speculated about the possibilities that the Hebrews had lived near certain of these monuments during their sojourn in Egypt. The result of Roberts' and Brockedon's efforts was a highly popular work and one that introduced many Englishmen to the architectural wonders of Egypt and Nubia.

# VI

# The Era
# of the First
# Professional Egyptologists

URING the period 1800 to 1850, Egyptology slowly began to evolve into a discipline restricted to professionals. When the nineteenth century dawned, all the major ruins in the Nile Valley had been explored, described, and sketched, and there was little original work left for the traveler who had not studied the hieroglyphic writing. A new type of investigator now appeared in Egypt. He was a scholar whose sojourn there was not a passing episode but a part of a lifelong study of the civilization and culture of ancient Egypt. In a sense, then, it was during the period 1800 to 1850 that the first professional Egyptologists made their appearance on the Eastern scene.

Perhaps the central figure in the exploration of ancient Egypt in the early decades of the nineteenth century was Henry Salt, an artist who served as British consul general in Egypt from 1816 to 1827.[1] In his spare time Salt collected antiquities. A number of field workers, including Giovanni Belzoni, an Italian, and Giovanni Athanasi, a Greek, looted the ruins of Upper Egypt to procure suitable objects for him. Salt sold many of these artifacts to the British Museum, and the French government paid a princely sum for at least one large assemblage. The collection remaining at his death was auctioned off to private enthusiasts.

Salt did far more than merely send out agents to collect antiquities. He also conducted his own excavations among the ruins, and after the works of Young and Champollion on hieroglyphic translation appeared, he spent much of his time copying hieroglyphic inscriptions and trying to decipher them. These researches into Egyptian inscriptions enabled him to add more hieroglyphic letters and names to the list then known, and in 1825 he published a defense of the new system of hieroglyphic translation.

Salt's early years in Egypt proved the hardest. To friends in England he wrote that "to stagnate thus at a distance from all science, literature, arts, knowledge, delicacy, and taste, is a punishment almost sufficient to drive one mad." Later he married an Englishwoman, and a happy domestic life combined with an increasing interest in his Egyptological work made him more content with life in Egypt. In a much later letter Salt informed an old friend that he spent all his time "ransacking tombs, poring over old inscriptions, and learning to decypher monograms, in which I assure you I am become very expert." He died in Egypt at the end of October, 1827.

Henry Salt's first agent, Giovanni Belzoni, earned for himself imperishable fame, as well as much notoriety, in the history of Egyptology.[2] Though a native of Italy, Belzoni spent much of his early manhood in England, where he performed as a strong man and as an actor. He had studied engineering during his earlier career as a Capuchin monk, and an effort to sell one of his inventions to the Egyptian government took him to Egypt. When the project fell through, Salt offered Belzoni a job that allowed him to use his mechanical knowledge.

For several years before 1820, Belzoni specialized in moving incredibly heavy objects down the Nile to Alexandria, whence his employer shipped them to England. Among other objects thus moved was the head "Young Memnon" that he found at Thebes. This huge bust of the Pharaoh Ramses II now rests in the British Museum thanks to Belzoni's skill as an engineer. Belzoni also led the group that cleared the sand from the temple at Abu Simbel.

Next Belzoni turned his attention to the Valley of the Kings near Thebes. After the fall of the Old Kingdom the Pharaohs had ceased to use pyramids as tombs. Instead, they had tunneled back into the high rock cliffs of this valley and used the tunnels as their tombs. Belzoni removed an immense pile of rubbish to reveal the entrance to the tomb of Seti I, of the Nineteenth Dynasty. This tomb was remarkably well preserved, though the Egyptians had removed the Pharaoh's body to hide it from grave robbers. Seti's body was found in 1881 in a cliff tomb at Deir el-Bahri in company with many other royal mummies.

Belzoni's methods of excavation were crude by modern standards; he even used a battering-ram occasionally. But he made an amazing number of important finds.

The 1820's were years in which Englishmen joined forces to explore the ruins of Egypt and the temples of the Sudan.[3] None of these men possessed greater love for Egyptological research than did Robert Hay, the wealthy heir to a great estate in Scotland. He is chiefly known as the leader of an expedition that explored, in a very systematic fashion, all the ruins of the Nile Valley in the years 1828 to 1839.

For this expedition Hay gathered together a crew, unrivaled in quality, of young artists and scholars. Among the members of this expedition were Frederick Catherwood, a famous painter of ancient ruins; Edward William Lane, the greatest Arabic scholar of the early nineteenth century; Joseph Bonomi, another artist; James Haliburton (called James Burton), an explorer and scholar; Francis Arundale, an artist; and Owen Browne Carter, an architect whom Hay employed to draw plans of the Egyptian ruins. These men later published accounts of their activities as members of the Hay Expedition, and some of them, particularly Bonomi and Haliburton, continued their Egyptological studies after leaving the expedition.

Bonomi had attended the Royal Academy in London, where he had studied under the famous architect Sir John Sloane. Sloane greatly admired the magnificence and gloomy grandeur of Piranesi's drawings of ancient Rome and introduced Bonomi to Piranesi's huge volume of Roman engravings. This influence is apparent in Bonomi's drawings of Assyrian and Egyptian ruins.

Bonomi made his greatest contribution to Egyptology through his accurate and tasteful reproductions of hieroglyphic inscriptions and of scenes on the walls of tombs. John Gardner Wilkinson and Samuel Sharpe, the most famous of the British writers about ancient Egypt during the early nineteenth century, selected from Bonomi's collection of paintings and drawings many of the illustrations for their books.

Robert Hay and his assistants began their work at Giza and Memphis in 1828, and by late 1832 they had surveyed all the ruins along the Nile into Upper Egypt and Nubia. On future trips, the expedition's members concentrated on sketching the ruins of certain sites along the Nile. During these years Haliburton, Hay, Catherwood, Bonomi, and the other members of the expedition began to look less like Englishmen. They smoked the long Turkish pipes and wore the robes and turbans of the Arabs. They even carried on much of their everyday conversation in Arabic.

Although Hay and his fellow workers compiled the most nearly complete record of Egyptian remains that had been assembled since the French expedition to Egypt in 1798–1801, little of the material was published. Hay wrote one book; a few of the drawings appeared in popular accounts of ancient Egypt; and other members of the expedition published several books. But the large volume of sketches, finished drawings, and travel notes which they had assembled remained in manuscript form.

The most famous English Egyptologist at mid-nineteenth century was Sir John Gardner Wilkinson, author of the best-selling *Manners and Customs of the Ancient Egyptians.*[4] This great book was the outgrowth of twelve years of exploratory work which Wilkinson undertook in 1821. Although he journeyed extensively throughout Egypt, fame came to him from his work in Thebes. Wilkinson built himself a comfortable dwelling on a hill above the Theban ruins and spent his days studying the pictures on the walls of the temples and tombs. He conducted some excavations, but he was far more interested in the paintings than in the objects and structures he uncovered. Although Wilkinson became convinced very early that Champollion's system of hieroglyphic decipherment was the only correct one and used it in his researches, he did not consider himself primarily a student of the Egyptian language. Rather, he studied the pictures in the tombs and temples in an attempt to discover all he could about the day-to-day activities, minor as well as major, of the Egyptians. Out of these studies he gathered the material for his book.

*Manners and Customs of the Ancient Egyptians* went through many reprintings and new editions in the course of the nineteenth century, and it eventually won for Wilkinson both a knighthood and a prominent position in the annals of British Egyptology. Through his reproductions of many Egyptian paintings, Wilkinson succeeded in presenting a huge amount of detailed information about the civilization, culture, and religion of the ancient Egyptians. He did not, however, seek to unravel Egyptian political history.

At last someone had decided to go to Egyptian rather than

classical sources for information about ancient Egyptian life, and *Manners and Customs of the Ancient Egyptians* remained the best account of Egyptian civilization until late in the nineteenth century, when scholars who had been studying the hieroglyphic writings began to publish more reliable information about Egyptian religious and philosophical ideas. Ironically, the faults of Wilkinson's book lay in the limited use that he did make of traditional sources. For example, he accepted unskeptically the biblical stories about the Israelites in Egypt, and he listed Hermes Trismegistus among the Egyptian gods. Even so, Wilkinson displayed more skepticism about traditional accounts than had earlier writers.

Although hieroglyphic studies were of little use to Wilkinson in 1837, they had progressed to some extent, and he was aware, for example, of such historical events as the religious revolution under Amenhotep IV (Ikhnaton or Akhenaten), of whose historical existence earlier scholars had had no idea.

Edward William Lane, the famous scholar of Arabic and associate of Robert Hay, spent about eleven years in Egypt.[5] Lane, a trained artist, introduced the use of a new instrument, the camera lucida, into the drawing of Egyptian buildings. With this instrument, which by means of a prism and a lens casts a small picture of a large object on a sheet of paper so that a draftsman can copy it, Lane obtained some remarkable drawings of Egyptian structures. He hoped to publish them in a projected work entitled *Exhaustive Description of Egypt*. He was unable, however, to find a publisher whose techniques of reproducing illustrations met his artistic standards and therefore refused to publish his work. Today Lane is remembered only as a great scholar of Arabic. His Egyptological activities have been all but forgotten.

By about 1830 explorers had drawn extensive plans of all the major ruins along the Nile from Cairo to Wadi Halfa.

They had also examined the ruins of the Faiyûm. But the ruins of two regions of Egypt and the Sudan had been neglected: the Nile Delta, whose cities remained covered with mounds of earth, and the area south of Wadi Halfa, where the pyramids and temples of the Cushite dynasties lay. The buried cities of the delta would not be unearthed until the end of the century, when Sir Flinders Petrie arrived, but the area south of Wadi Halfa received visits from two European explorers early in the century. The first was Frédéric Cailliaud, a Frenchman. The second was George Alexander Hoskins, an Englishman who had become interested in visiting the Sudan by reading Cailliaud's narrative of his travels.[6]

In early 1833, Hoskins proceeded by boat and camel beyond the junction of the Nile and Atbara rivers to Meroë, Gebel Barkal, and Nuri. Hoskins explored the pyramids at these ancient sites. All the portals faced the rising sun, and the Ethiopian builders, unlike the Egyptians, had used a true arch. None of the Nubian pyramids compared in size with the great ones in Egypt, however.

Hoskins had studied the new system of hieroglyphic decipherment, and he carried with him a copy of Champollion's recently published list of the Egyptian Pharaohs and their names in hieroglyphs. This list permitted him to identify the cartouches of a great many Pharaohs on the ruins above the Second Cataract, and the book he later wrote provided the first indication of how successive Egyptian dynasties had moved into Nubia.

Although Hoskins provided ample evidence that the Egyptians had penetrated into Nubia and the Sudan over a long period of time, he clung to the old belief that the civilization of Meroë had existed long before that of Egypt and that Egyptian civilization, and hence the civilization of the Western world, whose point of origin was then believed to be Egypt, had derived from that of the area around Meroë. This theory did not die until Richard Lepsius exploded it with his researches at Meroë and Napata in the 1840's, though even in Hoskins' time certain Egyptologists felt compelled to question it.

In 1842 the Prussian government sent an expedition to Egypt under the command of Richard Lepsius, one of the most influential Egyptologists of the nineteenth century.[7] From 1842 to 1845 Lepsius and his assistants made a careful study of the ruins in the Nile Valley, including those far south at Gebel Barkal and Meroë. The Prussian government later published the results, and this extensive report remains even today an important source for information about the Egyptian ruins.

Lepsius chose two Englishmen to accompany his German staff on the expedition. He took Joseph Bonomi along because of his skill as a copyist of hieroglyphs, and he also allowed James William Wild, an English architect, to join the expedition. Bonomi performed his usual skillful work, but Wild won greater, if short-lived, fame as the author of the "accretion" theory of pyramid construction, a theory Egyptologists now associate with the name of Lepsius.

Wild—and later Lepsius—tried to explain how a Pharaoh could build a pyramid in such a way that it could be finished quickly if he died suddenly. To do this, Wild decided, the Egyptians must have built a small, steep pyramid in the beginning and increased its size over the years by adding outer layers of stone to it, but leaving the top of the steep inner pyramid exposed. If a pyramid had to be completed quickly, the builders would stop adding outer layers of stone and add a small pyramidal structure to the exposed top of the inner pyramid. Then they would continue the steep sides of the inner pyramid to the ground by setting the casing stones into place from the top of the pyramid downward. Egyptologists long ago rejected most of Wild's theory, but some of its details, such as the adding of the casing stones from the top downward, may perhaps be valid.

By 1845 only the ruins of the delta awaited the first visits of explorers, but much yet remained for serious researchers to find out about the known ruins. Little excavation had yet been done, and few Egyptologists suspected the existence of prehistoric remains. In the last half of the century archaeologists would begin their work. However, the attention of Englishmen throughout the rest of the nineteenth century was not to be given to the tombs and temples, or to the possibility that prehistoric men had lived in Egypt. Instead, popular interest concentrated on those huge and mysterious monuments at Giza, structures that still held secrets for the clever and daring explorer to discover.

# VII

# Pyramid Explorers,
# Pyramidiots,
# and Some Obelisks

OR 250 years a steady stream of travelers had visited the great plateau of Giza. They had made substantial contributions to European knowledge of the structures there. They had drawn diagrams of the interior passages of the Great Pyramid, described the exterior of the two other pyramids, noted the locations of still other, smaller pyramids, and taken note of the mastabas. They had, in addition, discovered the remains of the temples, causeway, and walls that had been part of what might be called the pyramid complex. They had, however, little idea of exactly how the complex had looked when it was still intact.

Despite the successes of these travelers, much remained to be accomplished. Most of the relieving chambers, the subterranean chamber, and the ventilating passages in the Great Pyramid had not yet been discovered. No one knew where the well in the Great Pyramid might lead. The entrances to the pyramids of Chephren and of Mycerinus remained hidden under piles of rubbish, and no Egyptologist could say what chambers and passages, if any, the pyramids contained. The mastabas were still closed and their interior

construction unexamined. The catacombs of the plateau
had not been excavated. Finally, the old question about
whether the Sphinx contained interior passages that linked
up with underground passages connecting with the three
great pyramids needed to be settled. The explorers who arrived in Egypt at the end of the Napoleonic Wars began
clearing up these mysteries, and by the end of the nineteenth
century the work of many different men had found answers
to most of them.

On March 2, 1818, Giovanni Belzoni became the first
modern European to enter the second-largest burial monument in the world, the Pyramid of Chephren at Giza.[1] Pene-
trating quickly to the burial chamber, there he experienced
great disappointment. Since a huge mound of rubbish had
blocked the pyramid's entrance for centuries, he had hoped
to find intact the sarcophagus and the articles placed in the
burial chamber, but tomb robbers had long ago broken in,
stolen the objects, and emptied the sarcophagus. Although
he did not discover the rich find he had hoped for, Belzoni
did succeed in revealing the interior structure of Chephren's
pyramid.

In the 1820's and early 1830's the most extensive explorations at Giza were made by the Italian Giovanni Battista
Caviglia, a former sea captain.[2] Caviglia discovered the
passage that leads down to the subterranean chamber in
the Great Pyramid, and his workmen cleared the rubbish
out of these areas. In addition, he had them open the well
to the point where it connects with the subterranean passageway. Clearing out the well improved circulation inside
the Great Pyramid and provided the first hint that the well
had actually served as an exit tunnel for the builders who
had been charged with sealing off the King's Chamber.
When Caviglia stopped his work, only the ventilating passages and a few of the relieving chambers remained un-

discovered. The suffocating hot air of the pyramid's interior had seriously impeded his activities there.

Caviglia next ordered his Arab workmen to clear the sand away from the front of the Sphinx. Once this was accomplished, Europeans could gain some idea of the extensive complex that Chephren and later Pharaohs had erected around the Sphinx. Curiously, Caviglia believed that the Egyptians had built the Sphinx up from the ground, an opinion that has since been refuted. Today it is known to have been sculptured out of a natural outcropping of rock. Caviglia's work left the Sphinx exposed for only a short time; within a few years the sand had covered it again. In the twentieth century the Egyptian government again had the sand cleared away and has since, by almost constant effort, kept it clear.

Caviglia performed the first major excavations in the catacombs of the Giza Plateau. These rock tombs penetrate far back into the cliff. Caviglia cleared out one tomb to a distance of three hundred feet. Unfortunately, long before Caviglia's time tomb robbers had thoroughly plundered these graves, and only a few fragments of the original artifacts remained within.

Caviglia's researches revealed the interior structure of the Giza mastabas. Fragments of mummies and coffins which he found in the central chamber of each mastaba proved that the Egyptians had built these stone buildings as tombs. Some mastabas contained brilliant frescoes resembling those in the tombs of the Valley of the Kings.

A mass of new and important information regarding the ancient structures at Giza resulted from Caviglia's explorations, but his efforts had exhausted him and prepared him for his downfall. In February, 1836, Colonel Richard William Howard Vyse arrived at Giza, where he hoped to undertake explorations among the Pyramids. Knowing of

Caviglia's fame as an excavator, Vyse hired him to direct work on the second and third pyramids. In November, 1836, Vyse left for a tour of Upper Egypt and Nubia, leaving Caviglia to get the project under way. When he returned in January, 1837, he learned that Caviglia had not put the men to work on the pyramids but had them looking for mummies. Caviglia, convinced that the task of clearing out pyramids was too difficult, had decided to employ his laborers at an easier job. Vyse felt he had been tricked and was furious. The quarrel was smoothed over for the time being, but in late February, Vyse decided that he had put up with Caviglia's delays long enough and after a fierce argument fired him. Apparently Caviglia had simply been in Egypt too long and had become exhausted and nervous.

With Caviglia out of the way, Vyse proceeded to carry out the most extensive explorations of the Giza pyramids that had been attempted to that time. Vyse was a professional soldier descended from a long line of professional soldiers.[3] He believed in a literal interpretation of the Bible and displayed considerable hostility toward more liberal ideas. Convinced of the rightness of his projects, he was often impatient to secure results and willing to use unscientific and destructive means to gain them. Other explorers had speculated that the Sphinx might have passages inside. Vyse simply set up a drilling rig on the Sphinx and bored into it, failing to discover any interior passages. He thought that he might find additional relieving chambers above the King's Chamber in the Great Pyramid. Using gunpowder, he blasted out entrances to the three other relieving chambers. Egyptian workmen had carved hieroglyphs in these chambers. One of the inscriptions contained the royal name of Cheops and thus supplied the first direct proof that he had erected this pyramid. In addition, Vyse found the exterior opening of the ventilating passage leading from the King's Chamber to the pyramid's surface.

He then directed his laborers to the six smaller pyramids near the Great Pyramid and the Pyramid of Mycerinus. After forcing his way inside, he discovered that tomb robbers had visited the pyramids earlier but had left behind a few fragments. These badly damaged remains proved that at least some of the small pyramids had served as tombs for the royal princesses. A cartouche on the wall of a burial chamber testified that Mycerinus had built the larger pyramid nearby.

The Pyramid of Mycerinus next suffered assault by Vyse. The entrance passage to the pyramid was hidden by sand and debris. Burning with impatience, Vyse ordered the workmen to tunnel directly into the solid masonry of the pyramid. His expectation was that the tunnel would quickly meet an interior chamber or passage; then the entrance could easily be discovered by laborers working from the inside out. After digging into the center of the pyramid and then downward to the solid bedrock, Vyse decided that the passages and chambers must be subterranean. Using gunpowder again, he had the Arab workmen remove some of the granite blocks from the pyramid's base. This brought quick results. At the end of July, 1837, the laborers found the entrance.

Like the other Giza pyramids, that of Mycerinus had long before been pillaged by tomb robbers. The sarcophagus and some fragments of the lid lay in the burial chamber, but nothing else. Upon one of the fragments, however, Vyse found the cartouche of Mycerinus. There could no longer be any doubt about which Pharaohs had raised the first and third pyramids of Giza. Unfortunately, the ship transporting Mycerinus' sarcophagus to England sank at sea, and the sarcophagus disappeared forever.

The methods that Vyse used in uncovering the secrets of the Giza pyramids were rough. He inflicted permanent and senseless damage on almost every pyramid on the Giza

Plateau. Nevertheless, historians now take a much kinder attitude toward Vyse than they did several years ago. He was not a barbarian but rather a transitional figure in the history of archaeology. He used rough methods, but he kept a detailed record of his explorations and published it promptly for the benefit of scholars. In addition, he employed highly skilled assistants.

After he had returned to England, he continued to finance exploratory work among the Egyptian pyramids.[4] His agent in Egypt was John Shae Perring, a well-trained, experienced civil engineer. From 1837 to 1839, Perring carried out a truly scientific survey of the pyramids in Upper Egypt. He opened sealed pyramids and made careful measurements and drawings of several dozen pyramids south of Giza. He also made careful copies of all the hieroglyphic inscriptions he found in the course of his explorations. Later Samuel Birch, the leading authority on ancient languages at the British Museum, used the cartouches in these inscriptions to fix the kings in Egypt's dynastic history. For the first time Egyptologists knew in what order the Egyptians had erected the pyramids and could study their development. The hieroglyphic material also proved that the ancient Egyptians' attempts to restore old buildings had often led to the juxtaposition of newer structures with far earlier ones.

Perring emerged as the leading critic of the theory of pyramid construction set forth by Wild and Lepsius. Of the thirty-eight pyramids that he had surveyed in Egypt, Perring knew of only three that might have been erected in accordance with Wild's theory. Perring did not think much of Wild's abilities as a pyramid investigator because Wild possessed no knowledge of engineering. In his reply to Perring's criticisms, Wild asserted that as an architect he had as much right to comment on the structure of the pyramids as did an engineer. Nevertheless, Wild was forced to admit that the information then available did not lend much support to his theory, and he ended by taking the curious position that, while present knowledge of pyramid architecture did not support his theory very well, it did not disprove it either.

The published reports of Vyse and Perring were of great interest to John Dixon, another engineer.[5] In 1872, Dixon visited the Great Pyramid. He knew that Vyse had found an air channel, or ventilating passage, that connected the King's Chamber with the outside. An ingenious search of the Queen's Chamber led him to the discovery of similar channels ventilating this room. Egyptologists still refer to the two air passages of the Queen's Chamber as Dixon's Chambers.

By 1800, Egyptologists were certain that the Egyptians had used the pyramids as tombs, but during the course of the nineteenth century a multitude of cranks and cultists disputed the idea. Eventually professional Egyptologists would be able simply to ignore the various pyramid cults, but during the nineteenth century, they could not always do so. At least one pyramid cultist, Charles Piazzi Smyth, performed useful work in measuring the Great Pyramid at Giza and thereby made for himself an international reputation as an authority on the structure, origins, and function of the Great Pyramid. A multitude of other pyramidiots attracted considerable attention, scholarly and otherwise. The bizarre speculations concerning the pyramids had a long life, and at least one pyramid cult has succeeded in maintaining itself in the twentieth century.

The first pyramid cultist to attract widespread attention in the nineteenth century was George Stanley Faber, an author and a theological controversialist of the Anglican Church.[6] Faber's theories originally appeared in two works, *A Dissertation on the Mysteries of the Cabyri* (1803) and *The Origin of Pagan Idolatry* (1816). In these books Faber noted the striking similarities in shape, and to some extent in structure, among the pyramids of Egypt, the teocalli of

Mexico, the biblical Tower of Babel, and certain tumuli in Europe, Greece, and India. According to him, each of all these structures represented attempts to erect copies of Mount Ararat, upon which the Ark of the Old Testament had rested, and they were all dedicated to a universal god, worshiped under such names as Osiris, Thammuz, Iswara, and Hu. According to Faber, each of these structures contained a burial chamber—the symbolic tomb of the god— and had a flat place at its peak where priests could offer sacrifices.

Faber pointed out that the Egyptians had erected the Pyramids of Giza as tombs and that the Great Pyramid had a flat top. Belzoni's opening of the second pyramid had proved that it contained a burial chamber and a sarcophagus. The bones of a bull had been found in the sarcophagus, and Faber and his disciples cited this as evidence that the Egyptians had offered sacrifices to Osiris there. In 1819, Faber published a final statement of his theories: *Remarks on the Pyramid of Cephrenes, lately opened by Mr. Belzoni.* Faber's theories were very ingenious and, of course, completely erroneous, but Faberites continued to support his ideas after his death in 1854.

The superficial resemblance between the pyramids of Egypt and the ziggurats of Babylonia has always encouraged speculation that the Egyptians might have built the pyramids to serve as astronomical observatories. This hypothesis did not preclude the possibility of their having other purposes as well. In 1837, an anonymous author in *Fraser's Magazine* suggested that the Egyptians had built the pyramids as huge sundials and observatories, and a few years later Richard A. Proctor stated the theory of the astronomical function of the pyramid in its final form.[7]

In the years 1852–56, John Wilson, a writer on astronomy, published *The Lost Solar System of the Ancients Discovered.*[8] This book occupies a highly significant, if not very honorable, position in the history of pyramidiocy. Modern pyramid cultists have always maintained that in the measurements of the Great Pyramid at Giza are to be found many historical and scientific secrets. Wilson's book stated this concept in its earliest form. There was, however, one major difference between his book and those of later pyramidiots. Wilson insisted that not only the Great Pyramid but all the pyramids, obelisks, and temples of Egypt contained secrets in their measurements.

In Wilson's wildly bizarre book he claimed to have discovered a multitude of remarkable facts. From the measurements of the Great Pyramid at Giza he derived the distance from the earth to the sun, and from those of the Great Pyramid at Dahshûr, the diameter of Jupiter's orbit. From those of the Hypostyle Hall of the temple at Karnak he succeeded in determining the orbit of Saturn. The fact that his sources—the books of Greaves, Wilkinson, Vyse, and Perring—disagreed with his measurements did not bother him.

The next step in pyramidiotic speculation was taken by John Taylor, a friend of Coleridge and Keats and a minor literary critic. In 1860 he published a book on the Great Pyramid under the title *The Great Pyramid: Why Was It Built? and Who Built It?* In 1864 he published another book in which he replied to his critics: *The Battle of the Standards.*

According to Taylor, Holy Scripture contained references to the Great Pyramid in many passages; the architect of the Great Pyramid had not been an Egyptian but Noah, the designer of the Ark. Furthermore, locked in the measurements of the Great Pyramid were secrets of which the ancient Egyptians themselves had remained unaware. Among these secrets was the length of the "sacred cubit," identical to the cubit that the Israelites had used in biblical times. Taylor supplied "evidence" that the English system of measurement had derived from the "divine" system embodied in the Great Pyramid. Because many Englishmen admired Taylor's evident piety—and his opposition to the adoption of the French metrical system—his book enjoyed modest popularity.

Taylor's chief disciple and the real founder of the Great Pyramid cult was Charles Piazzi Smyth, the astronomer royal of Scotland. Smyth, an inventor known for his improvements in photography, became a convert to pyramidiocy after reading Taylor's books, and in 1864 he published a defense of Taylor's ideas: *Our Inheritance in the Great Pyramid*.

In 1865, Smyth, convinced that more precise measurements of the Great Pyramid than those available in published works were necessary, took his own scientific expedition to Giza.

Smyth was interested only in the Great Pyramid. The other monuments of the plateau he considered evil, pagan, and idolatrous. He spent his days making measurements of the exterior of the pyramid, its inner chambers and passages, and the sarcophagus. Smyth hated the tourists who came to Giza. He found them noisy and bothersome, and they forced him to suspend work for several hours each day. Above all, he felt that they did not show enough respect for the Great Pyramid.

Despite his strange ideas and misconceptions, Smyth performed much valuable work at Giza. He made the most accurate measurements of the Great Pyramid that any explorer had made up to that time, and he photographed the interior passages, using a magnesium light, for the first time. In 1867 he published the results of his efforts and his own speculations about the Great Pyramid in his magnum opus, *Life and Work at the Great Pyramid*.

Smyth's theories about the Great Pyramid exceeded those of John Taylor in grotesquerie. The Great Pyramid, Smyth maintained, was not an Egyptian monument. Rather, it was the oldest man-made structure; the other Egyptian pyramids were only filthy, pagan imitations. Although the Egyptians might have furnished the physical labor necessary to erect the Great Pyramid, the architectural genius who designed it must have been some personage of the Old Testament. The pyramid was a perfect structure, a product of divine inspiration, which embodied in its measurements a perfect system of weights and measures, among them the sacred cubit of the Israelites, the pyramid inch, and a system of prophecy. By use of the correct mathematical formulas, Smyth intended to unlock the secrets of the pyramid, secrets that included information about the past history of man, his future, and the Christian dispensation. He claimed that he had derived a number of astronomical facts, some dates of important events of the past, and a prediction about when the millennium would begin.

Many scholars published what should have been devastating criticisms of these theories. They showed, for example, that when deriving his formulas Smyth simply juggled facts and figures until he came up with a seeming correspondence and that many of the data upon which he based his theorizing, such as the average size of the casing stones that had once covered the Great Pyramid, were wrong. Contemporary Egyptologists knew that the Great Pyramid was not the earliest of the monuments, but one of the latest. However, pyramidiots were unswayed by facts.

Theories as bizarre as Smyth's inevitably produced a storm of criticism. What is surprising is the amount of support they received from reputable journals. Smyth responded quickly to all criticism. Shortly after the publication of his *Life and Work at the Great Pyramid* he produced an answer to its critics: *The Antiquity of Intellectual Man.* When the Royal Society of Edinburgh refused him permission to read a paper on the Great Pyramid in 1874, he resigned his fellowship in protest and published his reasons for doing so in a pamphlet entitled *The Great Pyramid and the Royal Society*.

During this controversy Smyth enlisted support mainly from two groups: the opponents of the introduction of the metric system into England and the antievolutionists. Smyth had stated in his books that the English inch was a close copy of the "pyramid inch," a perfect unit of measurement inspired by God. Hence, according to Smyth's reasoning, Parliament would be committing an irreligious act if it adopted the atheistic French metric system. Furthermore, Smyth continued to insist that the Great Pyramid was the oldest man-made monument in the world and hence that man had always displayed, with the Deity's aid, a high degree of intellectuality. These views were directly contradictory to theories of the evolutionary nature of man's development, a fact that the antievolutionists and Smyth clearly realized.

Richard A. Proctor, an astronomer, became the leading critic of Smyth's ideas, but unfortunately most of Proctor's beliefs about the pyramids were in their own way as bizarre as Smyth's.[9] Proctor also believed that the pyramids had never served as tombs. If they had, he explained, the Egyptians would not have found it necessary to build a pyramid for each Pharaoh. All the Pharaohs could have been buried in the Great Pyramid. He came to believe that the only theory that would satisfactorily explain why each Pharaoh had to build a new pyramid was one that took into account the astrological purposes served by the pyramids.

According to Proctor, each Pharaoh had erected a separate pyramid not as a tomb but as an astronomical observatory where the course of his life could be determined by astrological calculations. Proctor theorized that the people engaged in such work performed the observations not from the top of these structures—(an observer might get dizzy from being so high in the air)—but from the interior pas-

The Pyramids of Giza and the Sphinx, the first English view. From George Sandys, *Travels*, 1610.

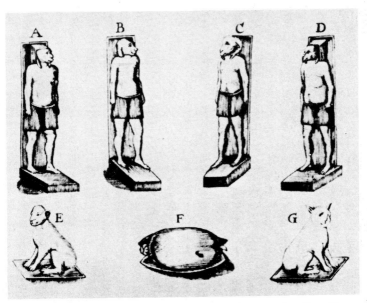

Egyptian statues of gods according to George Sandys. From George Sandys, *Travels*.

The steps and entrance to the Great Pyramid, the first English view. From George Sandys, *Travels*.

An imaginative reconstruction of an Egyptian temple, by an unknown eighteenth-century artist. The drawing bears only a faint resemblance to the probable appearance of an actual temple. From William George Browne, *Travels in Africa*, London, 1806.

Cleopatra's Needle and the fallen Alexandrian obelisk, as drawn by David Roberts, ca. 1838. From David Roberts, Rev. George Croby, and William Brockedon, *The Holy Land*, London, 1855.

Pompey's Pillar, as drawn by David Roberts, ca. 1838. From Roberts, Croby, and Brockedon, *The Holy Land.*

iew of Thebes, as drawn by David Roberts, ca. 1838. From Roberts, Croby,
d Brockedon, *The Holy Land.*

Obelisk at Thebes, as drawn by David Roberts, ca. 1838. From Roberts, Croby, and Brockedon, *The Holy Land.*

The colossi of Amenemhet III at Thebes, as drawn by David Roberts, ca. 1838. From Roberts, Croby, and Brockedon, *The Holy Land*. Classical writers referred to these great statues as the Colossi of Memnon.

The central avenue of the Hypostyle Hall in the Temple of Karnak, as drawn by David Roberts, ca. 1838. From Roberts, Croby, and Brockedon, *The Holy Land.*

The interior of the Temple of Dendera, as drawn by David Roberts, ca. 1838. From Roberts, Croby, and Brockedon, *The Holy Land*.

The temple at Ombos (Kom Ombos), as drawn by David Roberts, ca. 1838. From Roberts, Croby, and Brockedon, *The Holy Land*.

The Ptolemaic temple at Idfou (Edfou) before the earth was cleared from it, as drawn by David Roberts, ca. 1838. From Roberts, Croby, and Brockedon, *The Holy Land*.

The colossi at the entrance to the Temple of Ramses II at Abu Simbel, as drawn by David Roberts, ca. 1838. From Roberts, Croby, and Brockedon, *The Holy Land.*

The temple at El Dakkeh in Nubia, as drawn by David Roberts, ca. 1838. From Roberts, Croby, and Brockedon, *The Holy Land.*

Ramses III at play. From Sir John Gardner Wilkinson, *Manners and Customs of the Ancient Egyptians* (London, 1841).

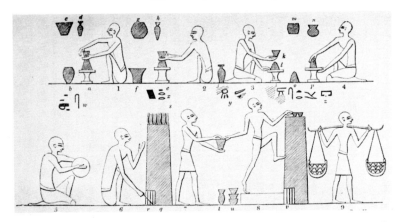

Egyptian potters. From Wilkinson, *Manners and Customs of the Ancient Egyptians*.

An Egyptian nobleman hunting birds and fishing along the Nile. From Wilkinson, *Manners and Customs of the Ancient Egyptians.*

"Chase of the Hippopotamus." From Wilkinson, *Manners and Customs of the Ancient Egyptians.*

"Joseph Interpreting Pharaoh's Dream." From Gustave Dore, *The Dore Bible Gallery* (Philadelphia, 1890).

"Embalming the Body of Joseph." From William Smith, *Illustrated History of the Bible* (Philadelphia, 1871).

sages. Each Pharaoh had his pyramid laid out according to the position of the stars at his birth. In addition, the passages of each pyramid had to be so built that they would be most useful in observing those heavenly bodies relevant to the life of the Pharaoh.

There were even wilder theories. Some people maintained that the Egyptians had built the pyramids as dikes to keep the sands of the desert from moving in and covering the cultivated area along the Nile. Others thought the Egyptians used the pyramids as places of refuge when the Nile flooded Egypt. Egyptologists had to wait until 1883, when Sir Flinders Petrie published the results of his explorations at Giza, to have an effective answer to these theories.

Next to the pyramids the Egyptian objects that attracted most attention—popular if not scholarly—were the obelisks. The nineteenth century witnessed a great scramble among the leading cities of the Western world for Egyptian obelisks. Paris was the first capital to acquire one, and before the end of the century London and New York had also done so. Private individuals also made off with them.[10]

The first Egyptian obelisks to reach England were two small ones, each about eight feet high, brought back by the British army in 1801 as part of the booty taken from the French. The obelisks had lost their pyramidions and pedestals and were cracked, but the hieroglyphs inscribed upon them were in good condition.

In 1819 a wealthy country gentleman, William John Bankes, hired Belzoni to transport a large obelisk from Philae to Alexandria. Bankes took the obelisk to England and set it up on his country estate. It was the first large obelisk taken to England.

Bankes made a useful contribution to Egyptology. While excavating amid the ruins of the temple of Ramses II at Abydos, he found a tablet containing a hieroglyphic inscription. It proved to be the first major king list entirely in hiero-

G

glyphs to be discovered. When it was deciphered, it furnished much information that was useful in fixing a more
nearly accurate Egyptian chronology.

The cause célèbre of nineteenth-century Egyptology was
the question of what would be done with the prostrate
obelisk that lay beside the standing obelisk known as Cleopatra's Needle in the harbor at Alexandria. The greatest of
the Eighteenth Dynasty Pharaohs, Thutmose III, had ordered the obelisk set up at Heliopolis, where it stood until
the emperor Augustus had it removed to the Alexandrian
waterfront. Eventually the obelisk fell down, breaking into
several pieces.

In 1801 the British army contemplated shipping it to
London but decided against doing so. In 1820, Mohammed
Ali, the ruler of Egypt, presented the obelisk to England as
a gift, but despite an intensive propaganda campaign in
favor of moving it to London, the British government refused to act. It would not be an easy undertaking—the
obelisk was a huge block of granite seventy feet long—and
it certainly would be an expensive one. Opinion was divided
on whether London should accept the gift. True, Paris had
acquired a large obelisk from Luxor, but should England
imitate an act that some denounced as typical French
vandalism?

Finally, more than fifty years later, Dr. Erasmus Wilson,
a wealthy London surgeon, agreed to finance the shipment
of the obelisk to England. The obelisk was so large and
heavy that an ordinary ship could not transport it, but the
pyramid explorer and engineer John Dixon solved the problem by building a large iron barge, in the shape of a huge
pontoon, around it. A steamer towed barge and obelisk to
London.

Early in 1878 the huge obelisk was set up on the Thames
embankment. The London weather promptly began erod-

ing the inscriptions. Nevertheless, its height and its massive thickness still make an impressive sight.

In the nineteenth century British excavators and explorers received much competition from French, German, and Italian archaeologists. As mentioned earlier, the German Egyptologist Richard Lepsius led an important expedition to Egypt in the years 1842–45. The French were the greatest competitors, however. In 1850 a young assistant in the Egyptian section of the Louvre, Auguste Mariette, arrived in Egypt. The directors of the Louvre had commissioned Mariette to purchase copies of Coptic manuscripts, but instead he used the funds to excavate the Serapeum at Memphis, the fantastic underground cemetery of the sacred Apis bulls. Mariette continued to make important discoveries until his death in 1881, and he performed an especially great service in supervising the establishment of the Egyptian Service of Antiquities. The service, a department of the Egyptian government was instrumental in preventing further destruction of Egyptian monuments by fortune seekers. Unfortunately for British archaeologists, Mariette used his position as head of the service to restrict drastically excavation by anyone who was not French, a restriction which earned him the hatred of many Englishmen.

After Mariette's death in 1881, Gaston Maspero, another Frenchman and the greatest historian of Egyptian civilization of his time, became director-general of the service. He permitted non-French archaeologists to conduct excavations and as a consequence became very popular among professionals.[11]

In addition to the major archaeologists and scholars, a multitude of lesser French, Italian, and German scientists invaded Egypt during this period. They examined the hieroglyphic inscriptions and excavated Egypt's historic and prehistoric monuments. The story of their adventures and explorations remains unwritten.

By the time the Alexandria obelisk had been set up in London, interest was shifting away from the larger Egyptian remains. Although explorers would continue to open pyramids and carry off obelisks, colossi, and other large Egyptian objects for several decades, archaeologists were becoming more interested in the significant smaller remains in Egypt. During the next half century, these new concerns began to assume prominence in the studies of Egyptologists.

# VIII

# Egyptian Archaeology
## at Mid-Century

HE second half of the nineteenth century brought improved conditions of travel for Egypt-bound Europeans. By 1872 steamships could take tourists in comfort from Italy to Alexandria in three and a half days. From Alexandria, a traveler could take a train to Cairo, making it unnecessary to endure the hazards of a boat trip up the Nile. The railroad ended at Cairo, but there he could secure passage on a small steamboat to Aswân and on to Philae. A tour of the sights along the Nile, which had taken three months in a dahabeah, could now be completed in three weeks. Travel by steamboat was also cheaper—and safer—than by dahabeah. At each important pyramid or temple the steamboat stopped to allow travelers to visit the ruins, and official guides were available to show them around. Back in Cairo, the tourist wishing to visit the Pyramids at Giza could hire a carriage, instead of a donkey as earlier travelers had done, and cross the new Nile bridge built by the khedive.

By 1862 the trip up the Nile had become so safe and comfortable that even the heir to the British throne could undertake it. In that year Prince Edward, the future Edward

85

VII, visited Egypt, and he made a return visit in 1868–69. Each time he toured the ancient ruins of Giza and Thebes.[1]

Of course, the steamboat tour had its disadvantages. No longer could the tourist make camp on the plateau before the pyramids. Nor could he spend as much time as he might wish among the ruins of, say, Thebes before continuing up-river. Whatever the tourist gained in comfort by taking the steamboat, he lost in the romantic experience of the trip by dahabeah. For that reason many travelers still preferred to hire a dahabeah and spend a season among the pyramids, obelisks, and temples.[2]

One such person was Archibald Henry Sayce, professor of Assyriology of Oxford. Sayce went so far as to buy his own dahabeah, and, beginning in 1879, he spent some seventeen winters in Egypt. The letters that he sent home to the popular magazines kept the British public informed of the work that archaeologists were carrying out in Egypt.[3]

Scientific exploration of the Nile Valley grew apace in the second half of the nineteenth century. The most important English archaeologist in the 1850's was Alexander Henry Rhind, who deserves recognition as the first scientific exca-vator of Egyptian ruins.[4] Rhind passed through life very quickly. Born into a wealthy Scottish family in 1833, he died of heart disease in Cairo in 1863, but he accomplished a tremendous amount of important work in his thirty years.

Rhind became fascinated by ancient history and archae-ology while attending public school, and his classes at the University of Aberdeen reinforced this interest. He soon became an enthusiastic antiquary and published frequent accounts of his excavations at various prehistoric sites in Scotland.

Rhind had long been interested in the Egyptian remains, but it was the development of a severe heart condition that prompted his first trip to Egypt in the winter of 1855–56. He believed that the cold winters of Scotland were too great a strain on his body and that the milder climate of Egypt offered him a greater chance for survival. Rhind began his excavations at Thebes, and in 1856 he published a work entitled *Egypt: Its Climate, Character, and Resources as a Winter Resort*, in which he gave some account of the Egyptian ruins. Returning home in the summer of 1856, he cleared out an ancient tumulus at Sibster, Scotland, and published a paper on the classification of prehistoric remains.

During the winter of 1856–57, Rhind was back in Egypt. The clearing of tombs in the Valley of the Kings took up most of his time, but his illness was such that it severely limited the amount of work he could do. Rhind spent the next few years in southern Europe writing papers on various aspects of Egyptian civilization. He also worked on the book upon which his reputation as an archaeologist rests, *Thebes its Tombs and Their Tenants . . .*, published in 1862. In the winter of 1862–63, he made a last trip to Egypt to study the alluvial deposits around the Egyptian temples. He planned to publish a book entitled *The Nile Valley in Relation to Chronology*, but his death in Cairo on July 3, 1863, put an end to the project. Samuel Birch and Andrew Leith Adams, Rhind's companion on the last trip up the Nile, wrote separate accounts of Rhind's final researches in Egypt.

Rhind performed his greatest services to Egyptology as an archaeologist. During the course of his excavations at the Theban necropolis, he displayed great persistence in the face of much disappointment and managed to uncover many hitherto unknown tombs. Excavations among the prehistoric ruins of Scotland had taught him the value that humble objects may possess for the careful investigator, and he was one of the first archaeologists to stress the importance of preserving the tools, weapons, and toys that were part of the daily lives of the ancient Egyptians. One of his most interesting finds of this sort consisted of "two wooden dolls, about twelve inches high with legs and arms jointed in the fashion most in request among denizens of modern nurseries."

Before Rhind appeared in Egypt, only one other excavator, Caviglia, had thought to clear a way into the mastabas on the Giza Plateau. Rhind opened one of the larger mastabas only to find that tomb robbers had long ago looted it. His account of the interior structure of the tomb was, however, far more precise than Caviglia's earlier descriptions.

In March, 1856, Rhind made his most significant discovery, a prehistoric grave near the Great Pyramid. This grave consisted of two parallel shafts, constructed of crude rubble work, descending to two burial chambers connected by a doorway. One chamber was empty, but the other contained rough pottery and a skeleton. The body had not been preserved and had been buried in a huddled position. Rhind had seen the remains of prehistoric burials all over Europe, and the similarity to those remains convinced him the Egyptian ones must be prehistoric also. Rhind was quite right. He had made a brilliant discovery, but few people at the time paid it any attention. Unfortunately, the jackals, hyenas, and dogs that roamed near his camp broke into the basket in which Rhind kept the skull of his prehistoric Egyptian and gnawed it "into rejected fragments."

Andrew Leith Adams, Rhind's companion on his last journey, was a geologist, naturalist, and archaeologist. On the trip Adams occupied himself with making a comparative study of the animals of ancient Egypt—as seen in the realistic pictures of them in the ancient sculptures and frescoes—and those of modern Egypt. Depicted among the ancient animals were several, such as the long-horned oxen, that had become extinct. Adams' *Notes of a Naturalist in the Nile Valley and Malta* remains today the best book on the animals shown in the sculptures and frescoes of ancient Egypt.

Rhind, meanwhile, was studying the alluvial deposits around Egyptian temples. He hoped that such inquiries would make clear the conditions of the Nile during past historical epochs, but his efforts proved much less productive than Adams'. Rhind was the first archaeologist to apply truly scientific techniques in his excavation work. He recorded his collections with enough detail that he could later distinguish among the remains of successive burials in the same tomb. He pleaded with other archaeologists not to tear apart the ruins to carry off large finds but to leave the ruins intact and make copies and photographs. Rapid publication of the results of excavations in such a form that other scholars could use them was a necessity, he believed, as he demonstrated in his book on Thebes. In his use of modern methods Rhind reminds the historian of the later explorer Petrie. Interestingly enough, like Petrie, Rhind received his earliest training as an archaeologist while studying prehistoric sites in Great Britain.

Shortly before Rhind unearthed the prehistoric pit grave at Giza, Leonard Horner, vice-president of the Royal Society of Edinburgh and of the Geological Society, had discovered a number of prehistoric remains at Memphis.[5] Horner had originally intended to study the alluvial deposits in Egypt, not to hunt for antiquities. He took with him to Egypt a number of drilling machines to collect samples of the sedimentary layers in the earth.

Horner made his most controversial discoveries at Memphis, where he began work in August, 1852. His boring device could extract only the smallest man-made objects and fragments of larger ones. Unexpectedly, the machine began to bring up pieces of pottery. At a depth of thirty-nine feet, it extracted pieces of brick-red pottery with a dark-gray interior. From depths between forty-five and fifty feet Horner procured fragments of bricks and additional pieces of pottery. He quickly realized that these Egyptian remains were older than anything previously discovered. He estimated that some of them dated back at least to 11,500 B.C. Although Horner's crude methods did not allow him to determine accurate dates, he had certainly stumbled across the remains of a prehistoric civilization.

At least one prominent Egyptologist adopted Horner's views on the prehistory of man in Egypt, but they aroused antagonism in other quarters. The antievolutionists were outraged: another scholar had joined forces with the devil and denied the biblical chronology. Orthodox journals denounced Horner's beliefs. But he survived the criticism, and in the next decade the explorations of Rhind and several French archaeologists confirmed his discoveries.

Sir John Lubbock, the greatest English authority on prehistoric society of his time, landed in Egypt in 1873.[6] Almost a decade earlier, in 1865, Lubbock had published *Prehistoric Times*, one of the most widely discussed scientific books in a century in which a great number of controversial scientific works appeared. It was Lubbock's book that popularized the term prehistoric. The terms Paleolithic and Neolithic also first appeared in Lubbock's book.

Lubbock intended his trip up the Nile in the fall of 1873 to be both a pleasure cruise and an opportunity to search for prehistoric remains. He took one of the scheduled steamships rather than a dahabeah—a sure sign that he was not going to work too hard—and made the usual tour of all the prominent remains along the Nile. At Abydos and at Thebes he selected likely sites and hunted for flints shaped into tools and weapons by prehistoric men. He assembled an impressive collection of prehistoric scrapers, weapons, plates, and other objects, and later, in the *Journal of the Anthropological Institute*, he published a description of them. Significantly, most of these objects turned up at Abydos, the site at which Petrie would, in the first decade of the twentieth century, unearth the remains of many prehistoric and early dynastic graves.

In 1872, shortly before Lubbock made his trip up the Nile, Richard Lepsius communicated to the Ethnological Society of Berlin information that he had received about the discovery of some prehistoric flints. The flints had been found at Helwan, a village about fifteen miles south of Cairo, on the east bank of the Nile, opposite Memphis. No one paid any attention to this report until a few years later, when the British geologist A. J. Jukes Browne decided to investigate the site at Helwan. Browne found extensive deposits of prehistoric flint flakes, scrapers, and knives. On December 11, 1877, he described his findings to a meeting of the Anthropological Institute of Great Britain.[7]

Captain Richard Francis Burton made the next find of prehistoric stone implements in Egypt. Today he is best known for his explorations in central Africa, his trip to Mecca, and his translation of the *Arabian Nights*. But Burton also performed important archaeological work in Asia Minor and, in 1878, in Egypt. Like Browne, Burton had read of Lubbock's discovery of prehistoric remains, and at Giza he began to search for others. He succeeded in finding a few prehistoric flint objects, and archaeologists whom he met in Egypt supplied him with others. In 1879 he published a description of them and a defense of Lubbock's earlier discoveries.[8]

Despite the exploratory activities of Horner, Rhind, Lubbock, Browne, Burton, and a large number of French scholars, little was determined about the prehistoric cultures of Egypt until Petrie began his excavations at Coptos and Abydos at the end of the century. Nevertheless, the earlier work on the prehistoric remains in Egypt, limited though it was, helped to prepare scholars for the discoveries that Petrie would later announce.

# IX

# Egyptological Studies and Egyptomania in the Nineteenth Century

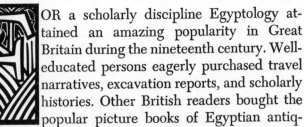OR a scholarly discipline Egyptology attained an amazing popularity in Great Britain during the nineteenth century. Well-educated persons eagerly purchased travel narratives, excavation reports, and scholarly histories. Other British readers bought the popular picture books of Egyptian antiquities, historical novels featuring Egyptian scenes, and pseudoscientific works by overly pious scholars trying to relate archaeological finds to biblical stories.

From what source or sources did all this interest in Egyptology derive? The Victorians were a serious-minded religious people—or at least so they appeared. Like their seventeenth-century ancestors, they believed the Bible to be a literal history of past events. Few incidents in the Bible attracted greater interest than the stories about the sojourn of the Israelites in Egypt. Much of the Victorians' interest in Egypt thus derived from the part which that ancient land had played in the sacred history of the Hebrews.[1]

There were, however, many other factors that contributed to the popular interest in Egyptology. Egypt occupied a prominent position in the works of the classical historians and geographers, and a knowledge of the classics was still considered indispensable for an educated man. The increasing ease with which tourists could visit the monuments of Egypt and the uniqueness of these structures encouraged educated travelers to visit and describe them. It should be noted that the interest shown by the British people in Egyptian studies was not unique. They displayed a similar, although not so intense, interest in other ancient civilizations —for example, those of Greece and Assyria. Finally, the discoveries made by Egyptologists and scholars from the deciphering of hieroglyphic writing and the prehistoric remains stirred interest and controversy.

Great progress was made during the nineteenth century in the study of Egyptian mummification.[2] Augustus Bozzi Granville, a physician and a student of Coptic, undertook the earliest nineteenth-century dissection of a mummy at his London home in 1825. From his detailed dissection he correctly concluded that the ancient Egyptians were Caucasians. He also succeeded in clearing up many erroneous ideas about the embalming process. Among other things, he proved the correctness of Herodotus' assertion that the ancient Egyptians had, when preparing a cadaver for burial, extracted the pituitary through the nostrils.

John Davidson, a physician and an explorer of North Africa and Mexico, performed the next significant dissection of a mummy. Davidson's interest in mummification— he had made a study of the embalming practices of people all over the world—led him to dissect a mummy of the Ptolemaic period. The surgical exploration, conducted in 1836, made it possible to correct some of the mistaken beliefs concerning mummification found in the classics. He established that the canopic jars, which the Egyptians had placed under each mummy, had contained the organs removed from the mummy, and he rejected the idea that a belief in the transmigration of souls had led the Egyptians to practice embalming. He drew some mistaken conclusions —suggesting that the Egyptians performed mummification as a re-enactment of the Osiris-Isis-Horus myth—and he lacked a sound understanding of the hieroglyphic inscriptions that he discovered among the mummy's wrappings.

The most authorative account of Egyptian embalming practices available to Egyptologists during the nineteenth century was Thomas Joseph Pettigrew's *History of Egyptian Mummies* (1834). Pettigrew was a skilled surgeon of broad interests and the author of many professional and popular books. Pettigrew first became interested in the Egyptian methods of embalming in 1820, when he assisted Belzoni in the unwrapping and dissecting of a mummy. From then until the end of 1852 he either assisted at or conducted regularly scheduled public examinations of mummies. Many of these exhibitions were attended by as many as six hundred people.

Gradually Pettigrew became interested in the broader aspects of Egyptology and archaeology. He studied hieroglyphic translation and made the acquaintance of such famous Egyptologists as Richard Madden, James Haliburton, and John Gardner Wilkinson. He intended to publish a compendium of all knowledge then available concerning ancient Egypt and its civilization, and in 1842 he published the first volume of the work, *Encyclopaedia Aegyptica, or a Dictionary of Egyptian Antiquities*. Publication of this first volume was paid for through subscriptions, but, unfortunately, Pettigrew was unable to obtain enough money to publish additional volumes. He participated in the founding of the British Archaeological Association in 1844, and became one of its most active members.

In his *History of Egyptian Mummies*, Pettigrew succeeded in dispelling much of the nonsense that many people believed about Egyptian embalming practices. It was widely accepted that the Egyptian embalmers had depended on magical formulas. Pettigrew established that mummification had been achieved by the total extraction of moisture from the body, and the interment of the body in a dry container, and the use of substances that resisted any moisture attracted by the body tissues. Finally, he stated that "the instances of natural mummies depend upon the same causes, accidentally existing, and brought into operation without the agency of artificial preparation." Thus he swept away many of the superstitions about Egyptian embalming.

Pettigrew actually succeeded in discovering many of the specific substances that the Egyptians had used in preparing a mummy. He agreed with Davidson that the Egyptians had placed the visceral organs in the canopic jars, and with Granville (and Herodotus) that the Egyptians had extracted the pituitary through the nostrils. Pettigrew offered no new conclusions about why the Egyptians had practiced embalming. He thought that they might have believed in the transmigration of souls or that they might simply have wanted to keep the bodies in good condition for some time before burial. Neither of these suggestions marked an advance over earlier speculations.

Although Pettigrew had left many questions unanswered, his *History of Egyptian Mummies* remained the best account of Egyptian mummification until the end of the century, when Dr. Grafton Elliot Smith studied mummies with more modern equipment, including X-ray machines.

Study of the forms of ancient Egyptian writing—hieroglyphic, hieratic, demotic, and Coptic—progressed slowly but steadily after Young and Champollion completed their decipherments.[3] The greatest Coptic scholar was an Anglican clergyman, Henry Tattam, who produced Coptic grammars and dictionaries and also translations of Coptic versions of the Gospels. James Cowles Prichard, an early ethnologist, published, in 1819, a barren work in which he tried to show a connection between the Egyptians and the

Hindus of India. Sir William Drummond, a British diplomat and student of the classics, wrote two works on Egyptian civilization. Drummond displayed some awareness of the work that Champollion had done in hieroglyphic translation. He recognized, for example, that many of the large temples in Egypt, such as the one at Dendera, were of comparatively recent date. In 1843, George Henry Wathen, an architect, published a book in which he stressed the importance of hieroglyphic studies in fixing an accurate Egyptian chronology, but his chronology was wide of the mark. Twenty years later an Oxford scholar, William Palmer, published a massive tome in which he attempted to correlate Egyptian and Old Testament chronology. In 1852, Anthony Charles Harris, a British commercial agent residing in Egypt, published *Hieroglyphical Standards*, an essay on the early history of Egypt. The work was of little value to Egyptologists; Harris did, however, make an important contribution by collecting papyri.

The minor figures in Egyptology mentioned above did little more than stimulate interest in the subject, but by the middle of the nineteenth century a number of British scholars were making significant progress in working with the language, literature, and thought of ancient Egypt. The first nineteenth-century scholar of major importance in the history of British Egyptology was Isaac Cullimore. In the 1830's he tried to establish a reliable Egyptian chronology. In a series of pioneering papers presented to the Royal Society of Literature, he utilized astronomical data and information derived from the newly discovered hieroglyphic tablets of Karnak and Abydos to fix the dates of the Egyptian dynasties.[4] In his later years Cullimore achieved a considerable reputation as a student of Babylonian cuneiform.

Throughout the nineteenth century Samuel Birch held the position of the foremost British authority on the lan-

guage, literature, and antiquities of Egypt.⁵ Birch rendered
his services to Egyptology as both a scholar and an adminis-
trator. In his youth Birch had studied Chinese, and in 1836
the trustees of the British Museum employed him to cata-
logue the collection of Chinese coins in the Department of
Antiquities. Later he turned to the study of the Egyptian
and other ancient Middle Eastern languages. Eventually he
was appointed assistant keeper in the Department of Antiquities, and he began a struggle, over the opposition of
fellow scholars, to secure a separate department for Middle
Eastern antiquities. First he divided the Department of
Antiquities into two departments, with the one that he
headed assigned Oriental, British, and medieval antiquities.
Later he became the head of the Department of Egyptian
and Oriental Antiquities. Part of the secret of Birch's success
was his long life. When he died in 1885, he had spent almost
fifty years in the British Museum, and all his earlier opponents were long dead.

Birch performed an immense amount of significant scholarly work and published the results in a multitude of books
and articles. When several critics attacked Champollion's
hieroglyphic decipherment, Birch was one of the first English scholars to come to his defense. He compiled many
catalogues of Egyptian remains in private British collections, made the first translation of the famous collection of
funeral texts known as the Book of the Dead, published the
best nineteenth-century Egyptian dictionary and grammar,
and wrote a history of Egypt. In 1870 he became the guiding
spirit in the movement that led to the establishment of the
Society of Biblical Archaeology. He served as the editor of
its series of translations of ancient texts—many of which
were Egyptian—called *Records of the Past*. In addition, he
performed much scholarly detective work using information
unearthed by archaeologists. Having worked with antiqui-

H

ties all of his professional life, Birch was an expert at spotting forgeries, and collectors often called for his aid in evaluating their acquisitions.

Acquaintance with a wide variety of languages and the ability to do creative scholarly work in decipherment and translation of inscriptions have always been characteristic of the successful Egyptologist. Edward Hincks, who lived all of his life in an obscure Anglican rectory in Ireland, possessed these necessary traits. Today Hincks is best remembered for his original work in deciphering Persian and Assyrian cuneiform. Long before he became interested in cuneiform, however, Hincks studied hieroglyphic decipherment and published articles defending Champollion's system. Throughout his life Hincks periodically returned to the study of Egyptian language and literature.[6]

Although he worked on clearing up the errors in the Egyptian chronology—a persistent problem for Egyptologists on which even today much work still remains to be done—and in translating the literature, he interested himself mainly in the development of the Egyptian religion. He was one of the first scholars to base his theories about the religion of the ancients almost exclusively on the hieroglyphic inscriptions. Hincks discussed the violent religious revolution of Amenhotep IV and the restoration under Harmhab (Horemheb), though the limited information that he could obtain from the texts then available prevented him from understanding the magnitude of that ancient struggle.

Over a period of several decades hieroglyphic translation gradually enabled scholars to recover the literature of ancient Egypt—the folk tales, legends, myths, and wisdom literature, and other forms peculiar to early peoples. Egyptologists recovered most of this literature from demotic and hieratic writings on papyri. One of the best-known scholars to work in this area of Egyptological research was Charles

Wycliffe Goodwin.[7] Goodwin became interested in Egyptology when, at the age of nine, he read an article on the work of Thomas Young and Champollion, and from then on it became the leading passion of his life. His interest embraced an amazing number of subjects. He learned to play several musical instruments; mastered the Greek, Latin, Anglo-Saxon, Hebrew, and German languages; and studied law. In his later years he served as a judge in courts in China and Japan. Despite the demands of these activities, Goodwin became Great Britain's finest hieroglyphic scholar.

In the volume *Cambridge Essays* (1858), Goodwin published an article entitled "Hieratic Papyri," designed to be a vindication of those who had defended Champollion's system. The essay revealed to the British public for the first time the wealth of ancient Egyptian literature in the hieratic and demotic scripts. It discussed the various translations Goodwin and other scholars, both British and French, had made from a papyrus in the British Museum.

This papyrus contained many of the now-famous classics: "The Tale of the Two Brothers," an account of the battle of Kadesh, "The Poem of Pentaur," "The Story of Sinuhe," "Instructions of Amenemhet I," "Maxims of Ptah-hotep," and "Complaint of the Eloquent Peasant." There were also many ordinary business letters that provided insights into the lives of Egyptian officials. Later Goodwin published an account of the "Story of Sinuhe" in a popular magazine and included this legend and others in *Records of the Past*, the twelve-volume work which appeared between 1874 and 1881. These translations provided irrefutable proof that hieroglyphic studies offered profitable new insights into the civilization of ancient Egypt.

While such scholars as these were making great advances in the study of the language and literature of ancient Egypt, other scholars were beginning to write the first significant histories of Egypt.[8] A popular writer on Egyptian history in the first two decades after the decipherment of hieroglyphic was Samuel Sharpe. Sharpe possessed some knowledge—not all of it sound—of both Hebrew and the hieroglyphic writing. He published many works, including reproductions of hieroglyphic inscriptions and a hieroglyphic dictionary, but the British public was most familiar with his two-volume *History of Egypt* (1846). This work marked no great advance over previous histories. Sharpe attempted to base his account of dynastic Egypt on information taken from hieroglyphic inscriptions, but, in fact, the standard classical works and the Bible were the sources of most of his "factual" information.

Though John Gardner Wilkinson's *Manners and Customs of the Ancient Egyptians* (1850) was the most popular book on ancient Egypt in the nineteenth century, John Kenrick's *Ancient Egypt Under the Pharaohs* (1850) was almost as widely read. Kenrick discussed the civilization and daily life of the Egyptians, as well as their history, and presented a summary of all that Egyptologists had learned. He made use of information from hieroglyphic inscriptions, and his chronology, based on astronomical deductions, was much more nearly accurate than earlier ones. Nevertheless, *Ancient Egypt Under the Pharaohs* was still based to a large degree on the traditional sources—although Kenrick did not accept the Old Testament stories as uncritically as Sharpe had done.

Christian Karl Josias Bunsen, Prussian ambassador to Great Britain from 1841 to 1854, spent much of that time writing a five-volume work, *Egypt's Place in Universal History*, which was published in both German and English. Bunsen's tomes differed little in content from those of Sharpe and Kenrick, except that he did accept the Egyptian chronology of Leonard Horner. In fact, he pushed the date of man's earliest presence in the Middle East and Asia back to 20,000 B.C. As might have been expected, the defenders of the chronology of mankind found in the margins of some editions of the King James Bible savagely attacked Bunsen's work. Bunsen wrote in such an incredibly dull style, and the complete set of his work on Egypt was so expensive, that had not the reviewers accused him of rampant heresy his books might have had only a very limited circulation. The attacks of the pious, however, succeeded in stimulating great interest in them.

The first accounts of ancient Egypt that foreshadowed twentieth-century histories in their almost complete reliance on hieroglyphic sources, their description of Egyptian literature and religion, and in their outline of historical events, began appearing in the late 1870's and early 1880's. The English translation of Henry Brugsch-Bey's *A History of Egypt Under the Pharaohs* went to press in 1879. In 1881, George Rawlinson published *A History of Ancient Egypt.* The basic outline of the major events in Egyptian history presented in these books does not differ from that of the latest mid-twentieth-century histories of Egypt. Both Brugsch-Bey and Rawlinson, however, accepted the historical validity of the Old Testament stories about the Israelites in Egypt, and they neglected to discuss evidence of prehistoric cultures in Egypt.

Like David Roberts' earlier work, *The Holy Land*, large, heavily illustrated books describing Eastern scenes, including Egyptian sites and ruins, were popular in the last half of the nineteenth century. An excellent example was *Picturesque Palestine Sinai and Egypt*, published between 1881 and 1884 in four lavishly illustrated volumes.[9]

As the nineteenth century progressed, Egyptology made an ever-increasing impact on the popular culture of England. Illustrated summaries of biblical stories were published for use by Sunday school teachers. Toward the middle of the century the artists who drew pictorial representations of Joseph interpreting Pharaoh's dream, Moses announcing himself to the Israelites, the Exodus, and other biblical scenes made some effort to draw in the backgrounds fairly accurate reproductions of Egyptian ruins. But these pictures were never truly realistic. The clothes and attitudes of the people portrayed there were utterly unlike those of the Egyptians.[10] Members of the Victorian middle class had little insight into the cultural life of a people so different from them, and they never really understood the ancient Egyptians.

Unscrupulous or unbalanced writers, including religious fanatics and racists, have always tended to pervert the sciences, particularly archaeology, to serve their ends. Among them were writers who tried to use archaeological "evidence" to lend historical support to the Old Testament narrative.[11] Around 1850, William Osburn, a member of the Archaeological Institute, published three books in which he tried to show that the scenes on the walls of the Egyptian monuments contained proof that the Israelites had lived in Egypt for a long period, as the biblical stories indicate. Osburn entitled his books *Ancient Egypt: Her Testimony to the Truth, Israel in Egypt*, and *The Monumental History of Egypt*.

Osburn refused to accept Champollion's account of the evolution of the Egyptian system of writing and came up with one of his own. He denied that the Hyksos invasion had taken place and declared Manetho's king list completely unreliable—conclusions that no contemporary Egyptologist would accept. He saw Israelites on Egyptian monuments where no one else had been able to do so, and he announced that an intimate relation existed between the ancient Egyptian and Hebrew languages. Finally, he believed that the Egyptians had originally resided on the Plains of Babel and that Cheops had raised the Great Pyramid as a faint imitation of that famous tower that was to reach to heaven. Although reviewers criticized Osburn's books unmercifully, a gullible public went right on buying them.

Religious publishing houses poured out a multitude of such books, of which the Reverend Henry G. Tomkins' *The Life and Times of Joseph in the Light of Egyptian Lore* may be selected as a representative example. Like most other writers of such books, Tomkins never attempted to prove by archaeological evidence that the Israelites had visited Egypt. Instead, he simply discussed what the Israelites had done in Egypt, using material that he had gleaned from the books of the German Egyptologist Georg Ebers, John Kenrick, J. G. Wilkinson, other famous scholars, and the reports of the Egypt Exploration Fund (see Chapter X) to fill out his narrative. Tomkins occasionally indulged in peculiarities all his own, for example, "translating" Hebrew words from monuments upon which they had never been inscribed.

In these years there was much commercial exploitation of interest in ancient Egypt.[12] Clowns used artifacts in their performances, and commercial museums of curiosities displayed Egyptian objects. One such museum was Egyptian Hall.

There also existed in many parts of England small private museums whose curiosities the public could view for a small fee. One of the best known, Joseph Mayer's museum in Liverpool, contained a large assemblage of Egyptian objects.

Another commercial venture was the panorama, the early-nineteenth-century precursor of the motion picture. It consisted of huge murals manipulated in such a way that scene after scene passed before an audience. The artist Frederick Catherwood painted many such murals of the Egyptian ruins at Thebes and Karnak.

What little effect Egyptology had on architecture during

the nineteenth century was mainly pernicious.[13] In the early 1830's, Edward James Willson, a London architect, drew up an extravagant scheme for a municipal cemetery in the shape of a pyramid. It would cost two and a half million pounds, stand two and a half times as high as Saint Paul's Cathedral, and contain 215,296 catacombs, with a capacity of 5,167,104 large coffins. At the rate of 40,000 coffins a year, it would take 125 years to fill it. The outside of this huge cemetery would be cased in granite with flights of stairs that could be climbed to the summit, from which an obelisk housing an astronomical observatory would rise. The pyramid would, so Willson believed, save the city an immense fortune in land that must otherwise be used as burial ground. As might be expected, the city government did not rush to build it.

Another grotesque architectural dream inspired by the popularity of things Egyptian was the mausoleum designed by the tenth duke of Hamilton, to be built on his family's estate.[14] Unlike Willson's dream, the duke's became a reality. He procured a beautiful Egyptian sarcophagus, decorated with hieroglyphic inscriptions, to hold his body inside the crypt. After Hamilton's death on August 18, 1852, Thomas Joseph Pettigrew embalmed the body and, with the help of several other men, deposited it within the sarcophagus. Then they placed over it the huge lid, designed to seal off the mausoleum forever.

Egyptology had a noticeable, though very limited, effect on the poetry, drama, and fiction of the period.[15] The "Head of Young Memmon," the bust of Ramses II that Belzoni removed from Thebes, may have inspired Shelley's "Ozymandias," and Lord Byron and John Clare alluded to the pyramids in their poems. In 1842, John Edmund Reade wrote a miserable drama entitled *A Record of the Pyramids.* The play was a Byronic parody having little to do with the realities of life in ancient Egypt. The popular magazines featured short stories whose scenes were laid in Egypt.

Toward the end of the nineteenth century two novelists whose books often contained Egyptian scenes attained great popularity with the English-reading public. They were Georg Ebers, a German Egyptologist, and Henry Rider Haggard. Ebers wrote most of his historical novels in the period from 1870 to 1900. Quickly translated into English, they sold very well. Readers were treated to stories laid in dynastic, Ptolemaic, Roman, and medieval times. As literary efforts, however, the novels possessed few merits.

Throughout his life H. Rider Haggard maintained an intense interest in Egypt and its ancient civilization. He visited Egypt twice, in 1889 and 1904, and toured the monuments and recently excavated archaeological sites. He acquired a library on Egyptology and collected Egyptian antiquities. Haggard wrote two historical novels, *Cleopatra* (1889) and *Queen of the Dawn* (1925), set in ancient Egypt, and many of his other novels contained references to Egypt.

It is possible that future historians may consider the rediscovery of the ancient languages, systems of thought, and literature of the Middle East of as great importance in the history of mankind as the recovery of the literature of Greece and Rome during the Renaissance. These discoveries of the nineteenth century forced scholars of the humanities to alter drastically earlier concepts about history, literature, and religion.

# X

# The Egypt Exploration Fund

Y 1880, Egyptology had developed into a highly specialized, respectable scholarly discipline, but archaeology, Egyptian or otherwise, remained an embryonic science. Although archaeologists no longer used dynamite to excavate sites, their techniques remained unrefined. Too many archaeologists concerned themselves only with big finds, and as a result they often destroyed many highly significant small objects during excavation. Indeed, a few archaeologists could still justly be called tomb plunderers. Except for the poorly supported and badly administered Egyptian Service of Antiquities, there was no permanent organization dedicated to promoting the systematic excavation of important sites in Egypt.

After 1880 all of this quickly changed. In that year Sir Flinders Petrie began his archaeological work in Egypt, and he soon succeeded in establishing the basic principles adhered to by all modern professional archaeologists. Two years later Amelia Blanford Edwards and her friend Reginald Stuart Poole joined with other interested persons to establish the Egypt Exploration Fund, a permanent organization that financed excavations in Egypt. Thus began modern Egyptian archaeology.

Amelia Blanford Edwards deserves much credit for both of these developments. She was primarily responsible for the establishment of the fund, and without its support during the early years of his work, Petrie, whose financial resources were limited throughout his life, could not have accomplished nearly as much as he did. In time Miss Edwards' efforts earned her the title the "first woman Egyptologist."

Although her lasting fame has derived from her efforts on behalf of Egyptology, Amelia Edwards first became famous as a popular novelist. Her first short story was printed in *Chamber's Journal*, and she regularly published articles and short stories in the popular magazines. Her first novel, *My Brother's Wife*, appeared in 1855, and from that year until she stopped writing fiction in 1880, she poured out novels at a remarkable rate. Although they were immensely popular in their day, none of them has survived the test of time. In 1880 she abruptly stopped writing fiction, despite the fact that her last novel had been her most successful.

The income from her novels supplied Miss Edwards with funds with which to travel. Her favorite country was Italy, and out of her Italian travels came material for her novels and her first volume of travel literature, *Untrodden Peaks and Unfrequented Valleys*, in which she described her adventures in 1872 in the Dolomites.[1]

Her travels abroad led her by chance to Egypt. In September, 1873, she and a friend, Marianne Brocklehurst, went to France to make some drawings. The weather proved to be exceedingly rainy, and so they debated the prospect of a visit to the sunny lands of the Mediterranean. After random discussion, they decided on Egypt.[2]

By her own testimony, immediately on arriving in Egypt

Miss Edwards became entranced with Egyptian antiquities and from then on remained fascinated by the remains of ancient Egypt. In fact, her conversion was perhaps not so sudden. She admitted that as a child she had read Wilkinson's accounts of ancient Egyptian civilization, Sir Austen Henry Layard's works on Assyrian Nineveh, and John Lloyd Stephens' account of the ancient civilizations of Central America. She had also read other outstanding works by important British and Continental Egyptologists and archaeologists. Whatever her earlier interest in Egyptology and archaeology may have been, she emerged from her trip up the Nile in 1873–74 committed to devoting her energies and talents to the promotion of Egyptology.

In 1877 she published an account of her journey, *A Thousand Miles up the Nile*, a work that is certainly one of the most skillfully written, entertaining, and enthusiastic travel narratives to come out of a voyage up the Nile, and it quickly became a best seller—and remained one until the end of the century. Her journey persuaded Miss Edwards that only scientific excavation could preserve the Egyptian antiquities from destruction by tomb robbers and amateur archaeologists. Several other people, Egyptologists and dilettantes, had also become convinced of the need to take action if the Egyptian remains were to be saved. In 1880 a group of concerned individuals, of whom Reginald Stuart Poole, an Egyptologist and head of the Numismatic Department of the British Museum, was the most prominent, met at the headquarters of the Society for the Protection of Ancient Buildings. They discussed a proposal to save the ancient ruins of Egypt, but nothing definite resulted from the meeting.[3]

Then Miss Edwards stumbled on the idea of the Egypt Exploration Fund. In March, 1882, with Poole's assistance, she succeeded in calling together the most famous Egyptologists of Great Britain. Meeting in the British Museum, this group of scholars and other interested persons formed the Egypt Exploration Fund. Sir Erasmus Wilson, the wealthy philanthropist who had brought the huge obelisk to London, contributed a large sum of money to the fund and was elected president. Miss Edwards and Poole became the secretaries in charge of a campaign to raise money. They also placed notices in newspapers about possible sites to be explored and arranged with Sir Gaston Maspero, director of the Egyptian Service of Antiquities, to have Egyptian sites opened for excavation by foreigners. The famous Swiss Egyptologist Édouard Naville accepted their offer to undertake the first excavation.[4]

The last years of her life she spent as a popularizer of Egyptology. In 1889–90 she made a highly successful lecture tour in America sponsored by the American branch of the fund. (It should perhaps be mentioned that some of the many women who were present in her audiences may have been drawn not only by an interest in Egyptology but also by the desire to see a defender of women's rights, another cause for which Miss Edwards had been active.) These lectures, published shortly before her death under the title *Pharaohs, Fellahs, and Explorers*, contained a popular account of Egyptology. Like most of her books, it was favorably reviewed and had good sales. She died not long after her return from America.[5]

Though Miss Edwards' contemporaries called her the "first woman Egyptologist," she would be more accurately described as a dedicated amateur Egyptologist with some literary talent and remarkable powers of persuasion. Unlike many amateurs, however, she was too intelligent to succumb to the bizarre and extravagant theories about Egyptian antiquities. She was a skillful and entertaining reporter, and she helped assure the future of British archaeology in Egypt.

Édouard Naville, the choice of the Egypt Exploration Fund to conduct its first excavations, was a colorful person and one of the most famous archaeologists of the late nine-teenth century. His home was in Switzerland, but he achieved fame in England, where his archaeological work was well known. Mariette, Lepsius, and Ebers were Na-ville's mentors in his exploration of the Egyptian remains. Naville never outgrew a dependence on the ideas of these three men. He became a determined opponent of anyone who discovered something that might alter the significance or interpretation of their findings. Hence he never accepted Petrie's discovery of the prehistoric remains in Egypt. The higher criticism of the Bible also drew his scorn. His highly conservative mind also refused to accept new concepts in archaeological techniques. By the time he started work, Petrie had begun laying down new rules for archaeologists. Petrie insisted that the small finds should be carefully pre-served. When studied and interpreted, they might prove as important as larger objects. Naville thought Petrie's theory was nonsense and made little effort to protect the smaller finds.

The Egypt Exploration Fund may have chosen Naville precisely because of his preference for the big objects and his religious conservatism. The new organization needed money, and impressive finds would make it easier to obtain donations. Too, some of the money at the disposal of the fund had been given with the understanding that much at-tention would be directed to the excavation of biblical sites. The fund could hardly afford to employ a scientist whose findings and interpretations might wound Victorian reli-gious prejudices.

Most of the early excavations in Egypt had taken place around the pyramids and in Upper Egypt.[6] In 1883 the Nile Delta was still virtually untouched by the archaeologist's spade. The Egypt Exploration Fund sent Naville to the delta, hoping that he would excavate the ancient site of Tanis. He arrived too late in the season to begin work there, however, and proceeded to another likely site, Tell el Maskhutah, which lay on the south side of a recently constructed fresh-water canal that ran from Cairo to the Red Sea port of Suez.

Tell el Maskhutah had become the subject of much scholarly concern. The French scholars who went to Egypt with Napoleon had proved that the site dated back to at least the days of Ramses II, and since then some Egyptologists had claimed the site lay on the route of the Hebrew exodus from Egypt. Richard Lepsius believed that Tell el Maskhutah was the site of Ramses, one of the two cities (Pithom being the other) that the Israelites were supposed to have built for Ramses II. In several articles published between 1880 and 1883, Amelia Edwards had defended Lepsius' opinion that Tell el Maskhutah was the site of the Ramses of the Old Testament. In 1860 the French engineers in charge of building the canal settled at Tell el Maskhutah, and they also called it Ramses.

Naville, for once disagreeing with the revered Lepsius, was certain that Tell el Maskhutah was not the site of ancient Ramses. A study of artifacts accidentally uncovered by the French engineers revealed that the Egyptians had dedicated objects there to the god Tum (Tem, or Atum). Naville concluded that the Egyptians had also dedicated the city to Tum, not to Ramses. The city's name would thus have been Pi Tum, and therefore very similar to, or the same as, Pithom. With this belief firmly fixed in his mind he started digging early in February.

Naville succeeded in uncovering a temple site, a wall, the remains of a city, a military camp, and a number of other structures. The remains belonged to a time span from the fifteenth century B.C. to the fourth century A.D. The evidence indicated that Ramses II had constructed the city, but nowhere in the city or camp could Naville find any direct evidence of the presence of the Israelites.

Naville always considered the excavations at Tell el Maskhutah his greatest work, and he never had any doubts that the site was ancient Pithom. The members of the Egypt Exploration Fund, needing demonstrable results for their campaign to raise more money, joined in a chorus of praise for Naville and his work at "Pithom." Many scholars refused to accept Naville's identification, however—some apparently doing so as a means of discrediting the Egypt Exploration Fund (one opponent complained that the fund contained representatives of every science except Egyptology).

The question of the identity of the city at Tell el Maskhutah has never been settled; opinions seem to vary in accordance with the scholars' religious beliefs. Nevertheless, Naville's excavations there supplied excellent publicity for the Egypt Exploration Fund. When the British public read that Naville had found the very walls that the Israelites had been forced to raise for the cruel Pharaoh, they were inclined to view the work of the fund very favorably. Once again science had been used to support beliefs put at the service of religious dogmatism.

# XI

# Sir Flinders Petrie
# and the Development
# of Scientific Excavation

NLIKE Édouard Naville, who repre-
sented the older school of archaeology,
the next excavator sponsored by the
Egypt Exploration Fund produced a veri-
table revolution in the methodology of
Near Eastern archaeology. Archaeologists before Petrie had all too often sought
large and esthetically pleasing finds, rather than those objects that could supply the greatest amount of useful information for the Egyptologist. They made little effort to record
carefully the manner in which they had altered the sites
they excavated, and they were oftentimes lax in publishing
accounts of their discoveries.

Petrie led the battle to alter these crude and unscientific
practices. He emphasized the importance of careful, slow
excavation in order to preserve small, fragile objects and insisted that seemingly insignificant objects, properly studied,
were often as important as much larger objects. He was the
first Near Eastern archaeologist to realize the importance of
fragments of pottery for comparative dating of sites; he developed a system of sequence dating for prehistoric remains;
and he urged other archaeologists to follow his example of

rapid publication. He trained younger archaeologists and published detailed and useful works on archaeological methodology. Through articles in popular magazines and books aimed at the general public, he worked to create widespread public support for Egyptological research.[1] Archaeology was a more truly scientific discipline after Petrie reshaped it.

While Petrie's new methodology was revolutionizing archaeology, his discoveries in the field were forcing Egyptologists to rewrite much of their reconstruction of ancient history. Among Petrie's discoveries were the city of Tanis, the Greek trading outpost at Naucratis, the location of ancient Daphnae, the pyramid of Amenemhet III, the prehistoric cultures at Qift, and the prehistoric and early dynastic remains at Abydos.

Petrie was born at Charlton, England, on June 8, 1853.[2] From a very early age he demonstrated an interest in ancient remains. When he was thirteen, he bought a copy of Charles Piazzi Smyth's *Our Inheritance in the Great Pyramid* and showed it to his father,[3] who was an engineer. William Petrie saw in Smyth's theories an admirable reconciliation of science and religion, and he wanted to do what he could in support of this reconciliation. He decided that he and his son should go to Giza and use their skills to secure even more precise measurements of the Great Pyramid.

To train for their work, William and Flinders Petrie practiced surveying Stonehenge, assembled a collection of surveying instruments, and read everything they could find on the antiquities of Egypt. In 1875 they published a book they had written on the measurement of ancient earthworks.

William Petrie was something of a procrastinator and kept delaying the trip to Egypt. Eventually his son had to go without him. That was probably just as well, for by this time Flinders Petrie had rejected the ideas of Piazzi Smyth.

Had his father been present at Giza, the probable clash of opinions might have hampered the work.

Petrie arrived in Egypt in December, 1880, and remained until the end of May, 1881.[4] While he was there, he restricted his activity to surveying, relying primarily on triangulation. In October, 1881, Petrie went back to Egypt, and except for a two-month trip up the Nile, remained at Giza until the end of April, 1882. During this second visit to Egypt he did some excavating.

Petrie's findings at Giza enabled him to disprove two prominent theories about the Pyramids, the accretion theory of Richard Lepsius and the belief of Charles Piazzi Smyth that the Great Pyramid was a product of divine revelation and, therefore, flawless. Petrie destroyed Lepsius' theory by showing exactly how the ancient Egyptians had constructed the Pyramids, and he also found much evidence that indicated the Great Pyramid contained imperfections resulting from poor construction and earthquake damage.

In examining the King's Chamber in the Great Pyramid, Petrie found that one or more earthquake shocks had broken every roof beam on the south side. Only the inward thrust of the massive walls held the four-hundred-ton granite roof in place. This damage had very likely occurred before the Egyptians had finished the construction, for mortar covered the cracks. Petrie believed that two architects had worked on the Great Pyramid and that the second had possessed much less skill than the first. The second architect had used rough stone and had often forgotten to dress the stone. The plaster applied to such areas failed to hide these imperfections. Petrie also found cracks that the workers had made in cutting the block for the sarcophagus. Charles Piazzi Smyth had noticed none of these defects.

Travelers in Egypt had long before noticed small temples that faced the eastern fronts of the second and third pyramids at Giza, but nobody had found a similar structure facing the Great Pyramid. In examining the basalt pavement on the eastern side of the Great Pyramid, Petrie noticed a number of granite and basalt blocks. He correctly reasoned that these were the remains of a large temple that had been connected to the Great Pyramid by the pavement.

At that time no one knew what purpose the Queen's Chamber had served in the Great Pyramid; they only knew that it had not been constructed to hold the body of a queen. Petrie's sharp eye for minute remains helped him devise a possible function for the room. He knew that in most pyramids there was a chamber called a serdab, which contained a statue of the Pharaoh. This statue, Petrie believed, served to receive the offerings made to the Pharaoh, while the Pharaoh's mummy rested in another room. Opposite the entrance to the Great Pyramid, Petrie found a number of small fragments of diorite, which the Egyptians had often used in making statues. Although the Queen's Chamber was empty, he had read in John Greaves's *Pyramidographia* that as late as the seventeenth century the Arabs had believed that the Queen's Chamber had once contained an "idol." He concluded the Queen's Chamber had been the serdab and that it had contained a diorite statue of the Pharaoh. This remains a possible explanation of the actual purpose of the "Queen's Chamber."

Another important discovery Petrie made at Giza was the ruins of a camp where the workers who had constructed the Great Pyramid had lived. He ascertained that the Egyptian workers had used bronze saws, which left green stains on the stone blocks, and diamond drills. He explained how the workers had moved the huge blocks into place by the use of stones, wooden beams, and a rocking process. Petrie made his only serious mistake when he tried to explain how the plug blocks had functioned in sealing off the ascending passage in the Great Pyramid, a problem that subsequent archaeologists solved, but Petrie made many observations that were of use to later investigators.

Ancient historians had attributed the construction of the second pyramid to Chephren; Petrie found the first definite proof of this identification when he discovered the cartouche of Chephren in the temple connected to the second pyramid by a causeway.

During his stay in Egypt, Petrie also explored the pyramids at Abu Roash, Saqqara, Dahshûr, and Medûm. He thought the Great Pyramid at Dahshûr equal to the second pyramid at Giza in grandeur and stated that limestone had once covered it as it had the Great Pyramid at Giza. The so-called Blunted Pyramid at Dahshûr, he noted, had once possessed a hinged door with bronze bearings on the south side. At Abu Roash he found piles of granite near the pyramid and concluded that the structure had once been encased in granite and lined on the interior with it. Petrie published the first description of the pyramid at Saqqara with rock retaining walls and an earth interior. He also visited the Step Pyramid of Zoser at Saqqara and noted the additions that had been made to it.

At Medûm he saw the tower-shaped pyramid often ascribed to Snefru, the first king of the Fourth Dynasty. He observed the rubbish around it and correctly surmised that this pyramid had once looked like the others but that the Egyptians had stripped off its outer layers, giving it a tower-like shape.

After comparing his findings at different sites, Petrie arrived at the conclusion that a great social revolution had swept over Egypt sometime during the period of the Old Kingdom. This upheaval had been marked by systematic destruction of tombs, sarcophagi, statues, and other royal relics. Clearly, those who had destroyed these objects had been consumed with a fierce hatred for the kings. Petrie imaginatively compared this work of destruction to the excesses of the mob during the French Revolution.

The survey of the Giza Pyramids was completed by Petrie at a fraction of the estimated cost. It was a remarkable achievement and made him famous as soon as it became known in archaeological circles. Aided by a grant from the Royal Society, Petrie published his findings in 1883 under the title *The Pyramids and Temples of Gizeh*; another edition of the book, from which many of the mathematical data were omitted, appeared shortly thereafter. Egyptologists greeted Petrie's work with praise. His measurements and observations provided them with the ammunition to sink the theories of Lepsius and Smyth.

Petrie's most enthusiastic reviewer was Amelia Edwards. Reginald Stuart Poole introduced the two, and Miss Edwards was soon convinced that Petrie was the greatest contemporary archaeologist. Henceforth she devoted much of her literary effort to publicizing Petrie's discoveries. When she died, her will provided for the establishment of a chair in Egyptology at University College, London. She named Petrie as her choice for the post, and he held it for over forty years. Petrie was not wealthy, and his position at University College supplied him with a dependable source of funds and assistants.

Petrie conducted his first excavations for the Egypt Exploration Fund between February and June, 1884, at Tanis, an ancient city in the delta.[5] The site consisted of a number of large mounds, which covered hidden cities, surrounded by swamps.

The number of men working for Petrie on the excavations at Tanis varied from 30 to 80. Petrie, unlike many other archaeologists, always treated native workers fairly and paid them enough that they would not be tempted to make off with finds they considered important. He also saw to it that his native overseers did not exploit the workers. The best laborers were selected by Petrie for work in those places where excavation was likely to uncover fragile objects. Instead of setting out simply to clear an entire area, a practice that he believed used too much labor and loosened too much earth, Petrie had the laborers dig trenches and pits in strategically selected places to see what they might reveal in the site. Further decisions about where digging should be done could then be made.

None of the discoveries Petrie made at Tanis profoundly altered the outline of Egyptian history, but he did find traces of two of the largest structures the ancient Egyptians had ever created, the temple and colossus of Ramses II.

Neither of these structures was standing when Petrie arrived at Tanis. Indeed, some centuries after Ramses II died, another Pharaoh had pulled down the colossus and used some of it in building a wall and gateway. When Petrie found the fragments of the colossus—and he never found more than a few of them—he did not immediately recognize them for what they were. But one of Petrie's major gifts to archaeology was the art of accurate mental reconstruction of past remains. He soon realized that he had uncovered the remains of a giant colossus, a structure larger than any of the other famous colossi. Petrie estimated that the complete statue might have risen above the ground about 125 feet and might have weighed approximately 1,200 tons. Not only had it towered to an incredible height but, unlike the other Egyptian colossi, which had been in sitting positions, it had stood in the hieratic attitude, with arms at the sides and the left foot forward. Constructed of red granite from Aswân, it had once been visible for many miles across the low, swampy land of the eastern delta.

Petrie's reputation as a pioneer in Near Eastern archaeology rests on more fundamental, if less spectacular, discoveries than those at Tanis. Among them were his findings at Naucratis during his next excavation operations for the Egypt Exploration Fund.[6] Tel Nebireh, the site of ancient Naucratis, was in the delta about midway between Cairo and Alexandria. Herodotus had referred to it as an important trading center for the Greeks in Egypt. Petrie went to Tel Nebireh in 1884 and remained until the spring of 1885. Ernest Gardner, Petrie's assistant and a scholar of Greek, helped him in the work, especially with the Greek inscriptions. During the second season, 1885–86, Petrie left most of the work to Gardner and went to Tel Defenneh (Daphnae). But most of the important discoveries came to light during the season in which Petrie directed the excavations.

Several distinct layers of remains appeared at Naucratis. The earliest consisted mainly of charcoal and ashes and might have been all that was left of an early Greek settlement or a pre-Grecian Egyptian village. The next town dated from about the time of Psamtik I, a king of the Twenty-sixth Dynasty. The Greeks had definitely moved into Naucratis by that time, and Petrie found there a crude mud-brick temple dedicated to Apollo. In the ruins of this temple a workman found the oldest Ionic volute ever discovered. Herodotus had mentioned five major buildings in ancient Naucratis, among them were a large Hellenion and an impressive temple of Apollo. Petrie's workers uncovered the Hellenion, a later temple of Apollo that the Greeks had built to replace the older one, and several other structures. They also found a temple dedicated to the Dioscuri (Castor and Pollux) which Herodotus had not mentioned.

The smaller objects, such as the Ionic volute, pottery fragments, and iron tools, that Petrie discovered at Naucratis stirred more excitement among Egyptologists than the remains of the buildings and temples. When a Greek of ancient times entered Egypt through Naucratis, he customarily bought a small piece of pottery which he gave to the temple as an offering to the god. The temples eventually became filled with statuettes and pottery vessels, and the temple officials removed them, broke them into small pieces, and threw them into a trench. When Petrie arrived on the scene, he found a trench filled with fragments of pottery. By carefully reconstructing them, Petrie and Gardner recovered many ancient inscriptions. Petrie also worked out a method of dating the artifacts in sequences.

Once they had established the Egyptian dates for these objects, which was easier to do than to establish the Greek dates, since the Egyptian chronology of that period was better known, archaeologists possessed a means of dating pottery made in Greece and on the Mediterranean islands by a comparative study of the pottery of Greece and the Aegean with that of Naucratis. Naucratis also supplied many answers to questions about commercial intercourse between Greece and Egypt in ancient times.

During the 1885–86 excavation season, while Gardner supervised the second season's work at Naucratis, Petrie excavated Tel Defenneh, the site of a Delta city that the Hebrews had called Tahpanhes and the Greeks had called Daphnae.[7] According to a biblical prophecy the Babylonian monarch Nebuchadrezzar was to destroy Tahpanhes because the Egyptians had given refuge to a fleeing Hebrew princess. When in 1884 the Assyriologist Archibald Henry Sayce reported that the Boulaq Museum in Cairo contained inscriptions of Nebuchadrezzar that Maspero had extracted from Tel Defenneh, interest in this area increased. Besides hoping to confirm the prophecy, Egyptologists expected that further explorations there would provide more information about the Greeks in Egypt during the reign of Psamtik I and thereby supplement the work at Tanis.

There were three large mounds at Daphnae. Two of them consisted only of rubbish, but the third and largest, which the Arabs called the Palace of the Jew's Daughter, contained the ruins of a large fire-gutted structure. Petrie proved that this building had been an enormous square tower that Psamtik I had constructed as a palace and a fortress for his Carian and Greek troops. Petrie found many Greek vases in the ruins and a number of bronze and iron tools and weapons. The vases and pottery were in fragments, but he succeeded in reconstructing many of them.

The most important of Petrie's finds at Tel Defenneh proved to be the Greek pottery remains. Like those at Tanis, these Greek artifacts threw much light on the history of both Egypt and Greece and on the development of commerce in the Mediterranean world. In addition, the excavations by Naville and Petrie opened up a new chapter in Egyptian archaeology—the exploration of the many hitherto neglected areas in the delta.

In 1889, Petrie found many other examples of Cypriot and Greek remains at Lahun, Kahun, and Tell Gurob in the Faiyûm. These foreign settlements dated back to Mycenaen times in Greece and perhaps earlier. Besides many potsherds he also discovered a cemetery containing the bodies of a people who resembled Homer's "golden-tressed Achaeans."[8]

In 1888–89 Petrie dug into a mud-brick pyramid at Hawara on the Nile.[9] At that time the king who had constructed this pyramid was unknown. When Petrie succeeded in tunneling through to the burial chamber, he discovered that once again tomb robbers had plundered the chamber and emptied the sarcophagus. They had, however, left behind a number of small objects whose inscriptions proved the pyramid had belonged to Amenemhet III of the Twelfth Dynasty. Petrie's work at Hawara supplied important information concerning the structure of the mud-brick pyramids in the Nile Valley.

Petrie made so many truly original discoveries that it is difficult to decide which were the most important, but certainly his work among the prehistoric sites in Egypt ranks very high on any list. Before Petrie, archaeologists had failed to uncover any sizable amounts of prehistoric artifacts in Egypt—partly the result of their disregard of the small, unimpressive, and fragile remains left by the prehistoric peoples. The effect of this one-sided approach was to make it seem that the Egyptians had suddenly appeared out of nowhere able to erect pyramids, establish an empire, and develop a complex civilization without any prior cultural evolution. All this changed when Petrie began his excavations in 1894 at Qift, on the western side of the Nile north of Thebes. Additional excavations at Deshasheh and at Dendera north of Cairo in 1897 revealed rich layers of prehistoric remains from a number of distinct cultures.[10]

When Petrie and his assistants first dug into the cemetery and townsite at Qift, they began to unearth large numbers of objects that did not fit any of the known facts about dynastic Egypt. The people who had inhabited the area had not embalmed bodies, and they had practiced ritual cannibalism. A fairly advanced culture had prevailed there. The people lined their tombs with wooden beams and fashioned tools and weapons out of copper and flint. They knew how to weave a kind of linen cloth, and they decorated the sides of vases with pictures of ships resembling the famous galleys of later days. At first Petrie thought these people were Libyan invaders who had arrived about 3000 B.C., but gradually he came to realize that he had found the remains of the first prehistoric culture to be discovered in Egypt. Probably other archaeologists, interested only in large, impressive finds, would not only have failed to recognize these artifacts for what they were but would never have bothered with such small and fragile objects at all.

Petrie's researches at Qift marked the beginning of a completely new development in archaeology. Within several decades archaeologists had discovered a number of prehistoric cultures, such as the Gerzean, the Badarian, the Amratian, the Tasian, and the Semainean. Petrie disliked the use of such vague terms as Early Bronze Age, Early Paleolithic Age, and Early Iron Age, in dating prehistoric remains. He developed a much more precise system, which permitted archaeologists to date a multitude of prehistoric cultures with great accuracy.

In 1896 Petrie made another discovery at Thebes of great interest to Egyptologists and to the general public as well.[11] Egyptologists had always been concerned with relations between the Israelites and the Egyptian Empire. Naville claimed to have found Pithom. Other archaeologists and scholars had found references to the Israelites in the Assyrian records, but no one had discovered any hieroglyphic inscription that mentioned the Israelites until Petrie explored the Theban ruins.

At Thebes, Petrie devoted his energies to exploring the remains of the temple of King Merenptah of the Nineteenth Dynasty. Among the ruins he found a large black-granite tablet on which several hieroglyphic inscriptions were carved. One inscription described Merenptah's victories over the enemies of Egypt. In a passage recording Merenptah's Syrian campaigns, the unknown author told how King Merenptah had utterly defeated the Israelites. At the time this discovery received wide publicity. It was hailed as another example of archaeological confirmation of biblical history. Few commentators noted that Merenptah had actually won his victory over the Hebrews beyond Egypt's boundaries in Syria. Hence Petrie's discovery did not really reinforce the biblical legend of the Israelites' sojourn in Egypt.

From 1896 until 1906, Petrie carried out a series of excavations among the royal tombs at Abydos that revolutionized theories about the earliest dynasties.[12] Tomb robbers had plundered these tombs in ancient times, and the medieval Copts had systematically destroyed as much as they could. Four years before Petrie arrived, French archaeologists had conducted excavations there. Petrie, whose otherwise pleasant personality was marred by hatred for his French rivals, accused them of doing almost as much damage to the site as the tomb robbers and the Copts had done.

From the wreckage Petrie unearthed an amazing variety of fascinating small artifacts. As in the case of his other excavations, he used great care and expended much energy in recovering fragile objects. An example of his workmanship can be seen in his search for the head of a statuette of Cheops. A workman brought Petrie a small ivory figure only three inches high. When Petrie cleaned it, he found one of the names of Cheops inscribed on it. No one had ever discovered a likeness of the king who had erected the Great Pyramid. Petrie knew that the head had probably gone with the waste dirt from the excavation. He selected the likely spots where the workers might have dumped it and then put his crews to work shifting the sand. After three weeks the head of the statue was found. It was no larger than the tip of a person's little finger. In working on the mud-brick tombs, Petrie used trowels and knives to cut away sections of the walls. Many pieces of ivory had been rotted by the surrounding organic muck that had formed when the wood in the tombs decayed. The ivory would disintegrate at a touch. Once, after observing several pieces of ivory embedded in a patch of ground, Petrie had the entire block of earth moved to his storeroom. After the earth had dried, he gradually took it apart with a camel's-hair paintbrush and extracted the ivory statuettes without damaging them.

Petrie's work at Abydos made it possible to trace the evolution of royal tombs from the predynastic mud-brick structures to the complex and often very beautiful tombs of the Second and Third Dynasties. He also filled in the blank spaces in the king lists of the earliest dynasties and discovered much about the predynastic kings, including some of their personal effects. Petrie's discoveries at Abydos demonstrated conclusively that there was a definite connection between the kingdoms of the First Dynasty, the predynastic kingdoms, and the prehistoric cultures. Here was proof that the mighty civilization of Egypt had developed from the simplest beginnings.

Petrie continued to conduct excavations until his death in 1942, but by 1906 he had established Egyptian archaeology as archaeologists now practice it. An entire school of scientists had been trained in his procedures, and many others had been influenced through his published works on excavation and archaeological methodology. He had opened up entire new areas of study by his discoveries at Naucratis, Daphnae, Qift, and Thebes and in the royal tombs of Abydos. Petrie became an archaeologist when archaeology was the domain of those who were little more than tomb robbers, and during his lifetime he transformed it into a truly scientific discipline.

# Abbreviations
# Used in Citations
# to Periodical Literature

| | |
|---|---|
| *AA* | *Archaeologia: Or Miscellaneous Tracts, Relating to Antiquity* (London) |
| *AC* | *Academy* |
| *AJ* | *Archaeological Journal* (British Archaeological Association, London) |
| *AJA* | *American Journal of Archaeology* |
| *AM* | *Atlantic Monthly* |
| *APSM* | *Appleton's Popular Science Monthly* |
| *AQR* | *American Quarterly Review* |
| *AR* | *Andover Review* |
| *ARRSI* | *Annual Report of the Board of Regents of the Smithsonian Institution* |
| *AT* | *Athenaeum: Journal of English and Foreign Literature, Science, the Fine Arts, Music, and the Drama* (London) |
| *BEL* | *Belgravia: An Illustrated London Magazine* |
| *BEM* | *Blackwood's Edinburgh Magazine* |
| *BQ* | *Baptist Quarterly* |
| *BQR* | *British Quarterly Review* |
| *CC* | *Christian Century* |
| *CE* | *Cambridge Essays* |
| *CEGR* | *Christian Examiner and General Review* |
| *CEJ* | *Chamber's Edinburgh Journal* |

| | |
|---|---|
| *CJPLSA* | *Chamber's Journal of Popular Literature, Science, and Art* |
| *CM* | *Century Magazine* |
| *CR* | *Contemporary Review* |
| *EMLR* | *European Magazine and London Review* |
| *EPJ* | *Edinburgh Philosophical Journal* |
| *ERCJ* | *Edinburgh Review: Or Critical Journal* |
| *FMTC* | *Fraser's Magazine for Town and Country* |
| *FQR* | *Foreign Quarterly Review* |
| *GMHC* | *Gentleman's Magazine and Historical Chronicle (London)* |
| *HMM* | *Harper's Monthly Magazine* |
| *HNMM* | *Harper's New Monthly Magazine* |
| *HW* | *Household Words: A Weekly Journal Conducted by Charles Dickens* |
| *JAI* | *Journal of the Anthropological Institute of Great Britain and Ireland* |
| *JEA* | *Journal of Egyptian Archaeology* |
| *JRGSL* | *Journal of the Royal Geographical Society of London* |
| *LA* | *Living Age* |
| *LH* | *Leisure Hour* |
| *LLA* | *Littell's Living Age* |
| *MR* | *Monthly Review* |
| *N* | *Nation* |
| *NAR* | *North American Review* |
| *Nature* | *Nature: A Weekly Illustrated Journal of Science* |
| *NBR* | *North British Review* |
| *NE* | *New Englander* |
| *NEM* | *New England Magazine* |
| *NMLAR* | *National Magazine Devoted to Literature, Art, and Religion* |
| *NMM* | *New Monthly Magazine* |
| *NQ* | *Notes and Queries* |
| *PM* | *Penny Magazine of the Society for the Diffusion of Useful Knowledge* |
| *PR* | *Prospective Review: A Quarterly Journal of Theology and Literature (London)* |

PSAS    *Proceedings of the Society of Antiquaries of Scotland*
        *(Edinburgh)*
PTRSL   *Philosophical Transactions of the Royal Society of*
        *London*
QR      *Quarterly Review*
RR      *Review of Reviews*
SAS     *Scientific American Supplement*
SM      *Scribner's Magazine*
SR      *Saturday Review*
STR     *Studies in the Renaissance*
TLS     *Times* (London) *Literary Supplement*
TRIA    *Transactions of the Royal Irish Academy*
URRM    *Unitarian Review and Religious Magazine*
WR      *Westminster Review*

# Notes

## CHAPTER I

1. Karl H. Dannenfeldt, "Egypt and Egyptian Antiquities in the Renaissance," *STR*, Vol. VI (1959), 7–8; Thomas Fuller, *A Pisgah-Sight of Palestine*, 77, 80, 82, 84; Peter Heylin, *Microcosmus: Or a Little Description of the Great World*, 387–97.

2. Dannenfeldt, "Egypt and Egyptian Antiquities in the Renaissance," *STR*, Vol. VI (1959), 8; Herodotus, *The Famous Hystory of Herodotus*, 156–58, 176–81, 183–86, 210–12, 224–26; Strabo, *The Geography of Strabo* (trans. by Horace Leonard Jones), VIII, 41, 87–97, 105–107.

3. Ammianus Marcellinus, *The Roman Historie* (trans. by Philemon Holland), 83–86, 211–16; Frank Cole Babbitt, "Introduction to Isis and Osiria," in Plutarch, *Plutarch's Moralia* (trans. by Frank Cole Babbitt), V, 3–4; Flavius Josephus, *The Works of Flavius Josephus* (trans. by William Whiston), 37–38, 62–76, 211, 766–68; Pliny, *Selections from the History of the World Commonly Called the Natural History of C. Plinius Secundus* (trans. by Philemon Holland, ed. by Paul Turner), 439–44; Plutarch, *Plutarch's Moralia*, V, 6–191.

4. Marcellinus, *The Roman Historie*, 216; D. Laertius, *Lives*, I, 225; Plato, *The Dialogues of Plato*, II, 223; III, 442–46.

5. Dannenfeldt, "Egypt and Egyptian Antiquities in the Renaissance," *STR*, Vol. VI (1959), 10; Erik Iversen, *The Myth of Egypt and Its Hieroglyphs in European Tradition*, 57.

6. Benjamin of Tudela, *Peregrination*, VIII, 586, 588, 590; Dannenfeldt, "Egypt and Egyptian Antiquities in the Renaissance," *STR*, Vol. VI (1959), 11.

7. Dannenfeldt, "Egypt and Egyptian Antiquities in the Renaissance,"

STR, Vol. VI (1959), 9–10; Hermes Mercurius Trismegistus, *The Divine Pymander of Hermes Mercurius Trismegistus* (trans. by John Everard), A2–A7; Iversen, *The Myth of Egypt*, 60, 83–84.

8. Samuel C. Chew, *The Crescent and the Rose: Islam and England During the Renaissance*, 85–86; Sir John Mandeville, *Mandeville's Travels* (ed. by P. Hamelius), I, 34.

9. Iversen, *The Myth of Egypt*, 62–63.

10. Francesco Colonna, *The Strife of Love in a Dream: Being the Elizabethan Version of the First Book of the Hypnerotomachia of Francesco Colonna* (ed. by Andrew Lang), 9, 13, 15–25, 35, 161, 235; Iversen, *The Myth of Egypt*, 62–63.

11. Iversen, *The Myth of Egypt*, 65, 70–77, 82–83.

12. Dannenfeldt, "Egypt and Egyptian Antiquities in the Renaissance," STR, Vol. VI (1959), 14–15; Africanus Leo, *The History and Description of Africa* (trans. by John Pory, ed. by Robert Brown), Vols. 92–94 of *Works Issued by the Hakluyt Society*, 1st ser., I, 17, III, 857–59, 867–68, 879–80, 896–97, 899, 902–904.

13. Iversen, *The Myth of Egypt*, 89–99.

14. Fuller, *A Pisgah-Sight of Palestine*, 88; Richard Knolles, *The Generall Historie of the Turkes*, 543.

15. Heylin, *Microcosmus*, 392.

16. Chew, *The Crescent and the Rose*, 4.

17. *Ibid.*, 86; Christopher Marlowe, *The Complete Plays of Christopher Marlowe* (ed. by Irving Ribner), 22, 37–47, 379–80; William Shakespeare, *The Tragedy of Anthony and Cleopatra*, in *The Yale Shakespeare* (ed. by Peter G. Phialas), 112–15.

18. Chew, *The Crescent and the Rose*, 85; Heylin, *Microcosmus*, 390; Knolles, *The Generall Historie of the Turkes*, 544; Shakespeare, *Anthony and Cleopatra*, 112–15.

19. Fuller, *A Pisgah-Sight of Palestine*, 74–75, 84–89.

20. Sir William Berkeley, *The Lost Lady*, in *A Select Collection of Old English Plays* (ed. by W. Carew Hazlitt), XII, 561; Richard Bovet, *Pandaemonium, or, The Devil's Cloyster* (ed. by Montague Summers), 18–19; R. R. Cawley, *The Voyagers*, 12–15; Chew, *The Crescent and the Rose*, 6; Kurt Karl Doberer, *The Goldmakers: 10,000 Years of Alchemy* (trans. by E. W. Dicks), 16–19; Fuller, *A Pisgah-Sight of Palestine*, 78; John Gaule, *Select Cases of Conscience Touching Witches and Witchcrafts*, 53; Joseph Glanvil, *Saducismus Triumphatus: Or Full and Plain Evidence Concerning Witches and Apparitions*, 291–96; Henry Holland, *A Treatise Against Witchcraft*, C1; Nathanael Homes, *Daemonologie, and Theologie*, 44–46; James I, *King James the First: Daemonologie (1597): News from Scotland (1591)*, 5; Reginald Scot, *The Discoverie of Witch-*

*craft*, 317–20; William Shakespeare, *Othello*, in *The Arden Edition of the Works of William Shakespeare* (ed. by M. R. Ridley), 127; Edmund Spenser, *The Poetical Works of Edmund Spenser* (ed. by J. C. Smith), III, 161; Arthur Edward Waite, *The Secret Tradition in Alchemy*, 48–54; John Webster, *The Displaying of Supposed Witchcraft*, 150–56.

21. Sir Thomas Browne, *The Works of Sir Thomas Browne* (ed. by Charles Sayle), III, 551–52; Chew, *The Crescent and the Rose*, 6; Dannenfeldt, "Egypt and Egyptian Antiquities in the Renaissance," *STR*, Vol. VI (1959), 10; Heylin, *Microcosmus*, 338; Iversen, *The Myth of Egypt*, 64–65; Ben Jonson, *The Alchemist* (ed. by Charles Montgomery Hathaway), in *Yale Studies in English* (ed. by Albert S. Cook), 157.

22. Francis Bacon, *The Works of Francis Bacon* (ed. by James Spedding, Robert Leslie Ellis, and Douglas Denon Heath), V, 153–54; Robert Boyle, *The Works of the Honourable Robert Boyle*, II, 451; Browne, *Works*, III, 141; Dannenfeldt, "Egypt and Egyptian Antiquities in the Renaissance," *STR*, Vol. VI (1959), 16–17; Fuller, *A Pisgah-Sight of Palestine*, 79; Shakespeare, *Othello*, 127.

23. Browne, *Works*, II, 185; Fuller, *A Pisgah-Sight of Palestine*, 77, 89–90; Heylin, *Microcosmus*, 387–94; Sir Walter Ralegh, *The History of the World in Five Books*, I, 20, 179–85, II, 59–69, 184, 225–27, 257.

# CHAPTER II

1. Dannenfeldt, "Egypt and Egyptian Antiquities in the Renaissance," *STR*, Vol. VI (1959), 23–26; John Evelyn, *Memoirs of John Evelyn, Esq.* (ed. by William Bray), I, 184–87, 194–97, 260, 669; *The Harleian Miscellany: Or, a Collection of Scarce, Curious and Entertaining Pamphlets and Tracts*, XII, 100–101, 105; Thomas Heywood, *The English Traveller*, B1; Leslie Hotson, *Shakespeare's Sonnets Dated and Other Essays*, 21–27; Iversen, *The Myth of Egypt*, plate VII, illustration 1; George B. Parks, "Introduction," in William Thomas, *The History of Italy (1549)*, ix–xi; Thomas, *ibid.*, 39–41.

2. This section is based on the following works: Sir William Foster, "Introduction," in John Sanderson, *The Travels of John Sanderson*, in *Works Issued by the Hakluyt Society* (ed. by Sir William Foster), xi–xiii; Richard Hakluyt (ed.), *The Principal Navigations, Voyages, Traffiques & Discoveries of the English Nation*, VI, 36–38, 43–45; Sanderson, *Travels*, LXVII, 39–50, 74–76; William Lithgow, *The Totall Discourse of the Rare Adventures & Painefull Peregrinations of Long Nineteene Yeares Travayles*, 14–15, 78, 110–11, 156–75, 198–99, 265, 274–77, 285–86.

3. Richard Beale Davis, *George Sandys: Poet-Adventurer*, 45, 60–62; Samuel Purchas (ed.), *Hakluytus Posthumus or Purchase His Pilgrimes*

*Contayning a History of the World in Sea Voyages and Lande Travells by Englishmen and Others*, VI, 183–85, 190–93, 195, 200–11, VIII, 103–104.

4. John Pinkerton (ed.), *A General Collection of the Most Interesting Voyages and Travels in All Parts of the World*, X, 222–23, 235, 239–43.

5. This section is based on the following works: Browne, *Works*, II, 360; Fuller, *A Pisgah-Sight of Palestine*, 84; Sir Alan Henderson Gardiner, *Egypt of the Pharaohs: An Introduction*, 11; John Greaves, *Pyramido-graphia: Or a Description of the Pyramids in Egypt*, A3–A4, 1–6, 16–17, 24–26, 28–41, 43–44, 47–51, 57–58, 67–77, 85–98, 102–15, 142; Robert William Theodore Gunther, *Early Science in Oxford*, XI, 48; Frederick Lewis Norden, *Travels in Egypt and Nubia*, I, 84–95.

# CHAPTER III

1. Leonard Cottrell, *The Mountains of Pharaoh*, 84–85; "Deaths," *Lloyd's Evening Post and British Chronicle*, Vol. XXI (September 28–30, 1767), 318; "The Great Pyramid," *NBR*, Vol. XLVII (September, 1867), 167; Robert Huntington, "A Letter from Dublin to the Publisher of These Tracts, Concerning the Porphyry Pillars in Egypt," *PTRSL*, Vol. XIV (July 20, 1684), 625–28; Iversen, *The Myth of Egypt*, 98, 106, 161; John Knox, *A New Collection of Voyages, Discoveries and Travels*, 179–80; John Nichols, *Literary Anecdotes of the Eighteenth Century*, I, 13–14; Richard Howard Vyse, *Operations Carried on at the Pyramids of Gizeh in 1837*, II, 217–20, 232–33.

2. Cottrell, *The Mountains of Pharaoh*, 88; *The Georgian Era*, III, 13–14; Gunther, *Early Science in Oxford*, XI, 131; "The Life of Thomas Shaw," *EMLR*, Vol. XIX (February, 1791), 83; Adolf Theodor Friedrich Michaelis, *A Century of Archaeological Discoveries* (trans. by Bettina Kahnweiler, preface by Percy Gardner), 284; John Pickford, "Thomas Shaw the Traveller," *NZ*, 7th ser., Vol. X (July 12, 1890), 28; Pinkerton, *A General Collection*, XV, 503–509; Thomas Shaw, *Travels, or Observations Relating to Several Parts of Barbary and the Levant*, 389–427.

3. Edwin Beresford Chancellor, *The Hell Fire Club*, Vol. IV of *The Lives of the Rakes*, 183; George Martelli, *Jemmy Twitcher: A Life of the Fourth Earl of Sandwich, 1718–1792*, 21–23; John Montagu, Fourth Earl of Sandwich, *A Voyage Performed by the Late Earl of Sandwich in the Years 1728 and 1739*, 395–96, 432–34, 452–60, 466–70.

4. James Baikie, *A Century of Excavation in the Land of the Pharaohs*, 91; Sir Ernest Alfred Thompson Wallis Budge, *The Rosetta Stone in the British Museum*, 189; Ahmed Fakhry, *The Pyramids*, 63–70; *The Georgian Era*, III, 16–17; Jacquetta Hawkes (ed.), *The World of the Past*, II, 447; Iversen, *The Myth of Egypt*, 109–10; William Mavor (ed.), *Historical*

*Account of the Most Celebrated Voyages, Travels, and Discoveries*, XIII, 1; Richard Pococke, *A Description of the East, and Some Other Countries*, iii–iv, 2–12, 17–18, 26, 29, 40–41, 46–66, 68–69, 73–123, 232–33.

5. Warren Royal Dawson, "The First Egyptian Society," *JEA*, Vol. XXIII (December, 1937), 259; Iversen, *The Myth of Egypt*, 108–109, Knox, *A New Collection*, 133–34; Alan Moorehead, *The Blue Nile*, 13; Norden, *Travels*, I, 5, 7–11, 23–24, 39–64, 70–79, 81, 96–98, II, 43–55, 58–65, 69–72, 82–96, 99–110.

6. Charles Perry, *A View of the Levant*, 311–15, 326–35, 340–51, 356–68, 372, 378–407, 419, 470–73.

7. Richard Dalton, *Remarks on Prints Intended to Be Published, Relative to the Manners, Customs, &c. of the Present Inhabitants of Egypt: From Drawings Made on the Spot, A.D. 1749*, 1–3, 15, 25, 29–34, 40–48; "Impartial and Critical Review of New Publications," *GMHC*, Vol. LI (September, 1781), 431–32; "Obituary of Considerable Persons, with Biographical Anecdotes," *GMHC*, Vol. XLI (February, 1791), 188.

8. Jonathan Curling, *Edward Wortley Montagu, 1713–1776: The Man in the Iron Wig*, 179–80; Dalton, *Remarks on Prints*, 41–47; Edward Wortley Montagu, "An Abstract of the Honourable Edward Wortley Montagu's Journey from Cairo, in Egypt, to the Written Mountains in the Desert of Sinai," *GMHC*, Vol. XXXVII (July, 1767), 374; Edward Wortley Montagu, "A Letter from Edward Wortley to William Watson," *PTRSL*, Vol. LVI (1766), 42–45; Edward Wortley Montagu, "New Observations on What Is Called Pompey's Pillar, in Egypt," *PTRSL*, Vol. LVII (1768), 438–41.

9. "Additions to Obituary," *GHMC*, Vol. LXXXVII (January, 1818), 93–94; *The Georgian Era*, III, 465–66; Eyles Irwin, *Eastern Eclogues Written During a Tour Through Arabia, Egypt, and Other Parts of Asia and Africa*, 7–12; Eyles Irwin, *Occasional Epistles Written During a Journey from London to Busrah in the Gulf of Persia.*

10. "Account of the Recent Discoveries in Egypt Respecting the Sphinx and the Great Pyramid," *EPJ*, Vol. I (1819), 89–90; Cottrell, *The Mountains of Pharaoh*, 92–95, 100; "Observations Relating to Some of the Antiquities of Egypt, from the Papers of the Late Mr. Davison," *QR*, Vol. XIX (July, 1818), 391–96; Robert Walpole (ed.), *Memoirs Relating to European and Asiatic Turkey, and Other Countries of the East*, 350–54, 358, 366, 379–80.

11. James Bruce, *Travels to Discover the Source of the Nile in the Years 1768, 1769, 1770, 1771, 1772, and 1773*, I, lxi, 40–45, 47, 53–54, 78–79, 91–96, 101–105, 107–12, 120–25, 138–43, 150, 156–57, 378–79, IV, 539–40; *The Georgian Era*, III, 36–37.

12. Browne, *Travels*, 14–32, 143–50, 177–84; *The Georgian Era*, III, 51–52; Pinkerton, *A General Collection*, XV, 108–109.

## CHAPTER IV

1. This section is based on the following works: John Frederick Blumenbach, "Observations on Some Egyptian Mummies Opened in London," *PTRSL*, Vol. LXXXIV (1794), 193; Edward Edwards, *Lives of the Founders of the British Museum*, 347; Nichols, *Literary Anecdotes*, III, 497–98; V, 333, 370–72; Thomas Greenhill, *Nepoxnoeia: Or the Art of Embalming*, 307–308; Pococke, *A Description of the East*, 213; Shaw, *Travels*, 424.

2. Warren Royal Dawson, "The First Egyptian Society," *JEA*, Vol. XXIII (December, 1937), 259; Joan Evans, *A History of the Society of Antiquaries*, 94, 158–59; Nichols, *Literary Anecdotes*, V, 504–506; Stuart Piggott, *William Stukeley: An Eighteenth-Century Antiquary*, 143; John A. Wilson, *Signs & Wonders upon Pharaoh: A History of American Egyptology*, 11.

3. William Guthrie, *A General History*, I, 2–237; Iversen, *The Myth of Egypt*, 102–103; John Jackson, *Chronological Antiquities: Or, The Antiquities and Chronology of the Most Ancient Kingdoms*, II, 64–402; Frank E. Manuel, *Isaac Newton: Historian*, 49–52; William Mavor (ed.), *Universal History, Ancient and Modern*, I, 150–212, II, 71–96; Sir Isaac Newton, *The Chronology of Ancient Kingdoms Amended*, 191–264; Charles Rollin, *The Ancient History of the Egyptians, Carthaginians, Assyrians, Babylonians, Medes and Persians, Grecians and Macedonians* (trans. by R. Lynam), I, 117–88.

4. Budge, *The Rosetta Stone*, 189; Robert Chambers, *A Biographical Dictionary of Eminent Scotsmen*, II, 254, 454–55; Nichols, *Literary Anecdotes*, V, 329–37; John Woodward and Michael Lord, "Of the Wisdom of the Antient Egyptians: A Discourse Concerning Their Arts, Their Sciences, and Their Learning," *AA*, Vol. IV (1786), 212–310.

5. This section is based on the following works: Budge, *The Rosetta Stone*, 190–91; Robert Clayton, *A Journal from Grand Cairo to Mount Sinai, and Back Again: To Which Are Added Remarks on the Origin of Hieroglyphics*, 55–59; Henry Coventry, *Philemon to Pydaspes: Or, The History of False Religion in the Earlier Pagan World*, 299–300, 304, 309, 312–15; Curling, *Edward Wortley Montagu*, 164–67; "Extract from the Journals of the Royal Society, June 23, 1768, Respecting a Letter Addressed to the Society by a Member of the House of Jesuits at Pekin in China," *PTRSL*, Vol. LVIV (1770), 459–95; *The Georgian Era*, III, 483; Iversen, *The Myth of Egypt*, 103–107; Manuel, *Isaac Newton*, 181; Nichols, *Literary Anecdotes*, I, 618–19, II, 165–66, V, 564–67, VIII, 230; Pococke, *A Description of the East*, 227–30; William Warburton, *The Divine Legation*, II, part 1, 66–206.

6. This section is based on the following works: Blumenbach, "Observations on Some Egyptian Mummies Opened in London," *PTRSL*, Vol.

LXXIV (1794), 178–94; A. B. Glanville, "An Essay on Egyptian Mummies: With Observations on the Art of Embalming Among the Ancient Egyptians," *PTRSL*, Vol. CXV, part 1 (1825), 282–86; Greenhill, *Nepoxnoeia*, 20–308, 330–67; John Hadley, "An Account of a Mummy, Inspected at London 1763," *PTRSL*, Vol. LIV (1764), 1–14.

7. Glyn Edmund Daniel, *The Idea of Prehistory*, 30; "The Great Pyramid," *NBR*, Vol. XLVII (September, 1867), 184; Frederick Samuel Schmidt, "Dissertation Littéraire sur une Colonie Égiptienne etablié à Athènes: Presentée a l'illustré Acádemie des Antiquaires de Londres," *AA*, Vol. I (1779), 240–61; Charles Vallancy, *An Essay on the Antiquity of the Irish Language*.

8. H. F. Clark, *The English Landscape Garden*, 37–40, 55–57; Iversen, *The Myth of Egypt*, 102, 121–22, 162; Nigel Nicolson, *Great Houses of Britain*, 181–83, 230–37; Brian Tunstall, *William Pitt, Earl of Chatham*, 87–88.

# CHAPTER V

1. This section is based on the following works: "Appendix. Inscriptions," *AA*, Vol. XV (1806), 389; Baikie, *A Century of Excavation*, 7–8; Budge, *The Rosetta Stone*, 28–29; Edward Daniel Clarke, *The Tomb of Alexander*, 25–95; Edward Daniel Clarke, *Travels in Various Countries of Europe, Asia and Africa*, II, 264–99, 304, 493–97, III, 185–91, 208–99, IV, 98–175; Francis Collins, *Voyages to Portugal, Spain, Sicily, Malta, Asia-Minor, Egypt, &c. &c. from 1796 to 1801*, 132–35, 148; "Cromlech near Mount Orgueil Castle, in Jersey," *AA*, Vol. XXVIII (1840), 461; Edwards, *Lives*, 363–68; Evans, *A History of the Society of Antiquaries*, 199–200; "Hamilton's Aegyptica," *ERCJ*, Vol. XVIII (August, 1811), 437–44; J. Christopher Herold, *Bonaparte in Egypt*; Iversen, *The Myth of Egypt*, 128; William Otter, *The Life and Remains of the Reverend Edward Daniel Clarke*, 45, 84–140, 334–495, 543–47; Matthew Roper, "An Account of the Rosetta Stone, in Three Languages, Which Was Brought to England in the Year 1802," *AA*, Vol. XVI (1812), 207–11; Tomkyns Hilgrove Turner, "An Account of the Rosetta Stone," *AA*, Vol. XVI (1812), 212–14; Wilson, *Signs & Wonders upon Pharaoh*, 14–17.

2. Dominique Francois Jean Arago, "Eulogy on Thomas Young," *ARRSI* (1872), 129; Budge, *The Rosetta Stone*, 129, 197–201; "Cory's Ancient Fragments, &c.," *BEM*, Vol. XLIV (October, 1838), 105–106; Glyn Edmund Daniel, *A Hundred Years of Archaeology*, 68; Robert Deverell, *Andalusia; Or, Notes Tending to Show that the Yellow Fever of the West Indies, and of Andalusia in Spain, Was a Disease Well Known to the Ancients*, 70, 119–38; Robert Deverell, *A Supplement to Notes on the Ancient Method of Treating the Fever of Andalusia, Now Called the*

*Yellow Fever; Deduced from an Explanation of the Hieroglyphics Painted upon the Cambridge Mummy*, 2, 5–40; William Richard Hamilton, "Some Account of the Egyptian Papyrus and the Mode Adapted for Unfolding a Roll of the Same," *AA*, Vol. XVI (1812), 173–74; "Hieroglyphics," *ERCJ*, Vol. XLV (December, 1826), 107, 112–13; Iversen, *The Myth of Egypt*, 128–30; Alexander Wood and Frank Oldham, *Thomas Young: Natural Philosopher, 1773–1829*, 208.

3. The material on Thomas Young was derived from the following works: Arago, "Eulogy on Thomas Young," *ARRSI* (1872), 131–33; Sir William Edward Rouse Boughton, "A Letter from W. E. Rouse Boughton, to the Reverend Stephen Watson," *AA*, Vol. XVIII (1817), 59–60; Budge, *The Rosetta Stone*, 199–214; C. W. Ceram, *The March of Archaeology* (trans. by Richard and Clara Winston), 86; "Cory's Ancient Fragments, &c.," *BEM*, Vol. XLIV (October, 1838), 106; Iversen, *The Myth of Egypt*, 134–37, 141–42; "Klaproth on Hieroglyphical Discovery," *ERCJ*, Vol. LVII (July, 1833), 464–66; "Manners and Customs of the Ancient Egyptians," *ERCJ*, Vol. CXXXVIII (January, 1839), 334–37; "Salt's Essay on Phonetic Hieroglyphics," *MR*, Vol. XVII (1825), 177–79; Henry Salt, *Essay on Dr. Young's and M. Champollion's Phonetic System of Hieroglyphics*, 1–3; "System of Phonetic Hieroglyphs," *WR*, Vol. IV (July, 1825), 41–42; Wilson, *Signs & Wonders upon Pharaoh*, 18; Wood and Oldham, *Thomas Young*, 208–55.

4. "Brugsch's Egypt Under the Pharaohs," *ERCJ*, Vol. CL (July, 1879), 78, 110; "The Definite Results of Egyptology," *N*, Vol. V (July 4, 1867), 5; "Further Notices of Hieroglyphics," *ERCJ*, Vol. XLV (March, 1927), 528–30; Charles Wycliffe Goodwin, "Hieratic Papyri," *CE* (1858), 228–29; "Hieroglyphics," *FQR*, Vol. IV (August, 1829), 438, 453–57; "Hieroglyphic and Cuneiform Interpretation," *QR*, Vol. CXLVII (April, 1879), 434; Sir George Cornewall Lewis, *An Historicall Survey of the Astronomy of the Ancients*; William Mure, *Brief Remarks on the Chronology of the Egyptian Dynasties*; "The New Pharonic Tablets of Memphis and Abydos," *BQR*, Vol. XLI (January, 1865), 170–81; "Recent Works on Egyptology," *NAR*, Vol. XCVI (January, 1883), 111–16; "Wall on Egyptian Hieroglyphs, and on the Origin of Alphabetic Writing," *ERCJ*, Vol. LXIV (October, 1836), 43; Charles William Wall, *An Examination of the Ancient Orthography of the Jews with Which Is Incorporated an Essay on Egyptian Hieroglyphs*; Wilson, *Signs & Wonders upon Pharaoh*, 19.

5. The material on Legh, Buckingham, Light, Belmore, Edmonstone, Waddington, and Hanbury has been taken from the following works: Sir Ernest Alfred Thompson Wallis Budge, *The Egyptian Sudan: Its History and Monuments*, I, 34–38; The Georgian Era, III, 70–84; John James Halls, *The Life and Correspondence of Henry Salt, Esq.*, 43–47; Thomas Legh, *Narrative of a Journey in Egypt and the Country Beyond the Cataracts*, v–vi, 51, 62, 65–67, 75–88, 91–93, 97–98; Moorehead, *The Blue Nile*,

142–44; Ralph E. Turner, *James Silk Buckingham, 1786–1855: A Social Biography*, 71–84; Walpole, *Memoirs*, 407–29.

6. Moorehead, *The Blue Nile*, 144–66; Otter, *Life of Edward Daniel Clarke*, 584, 603–19; Wilson, *Signs & Wonders upon Pharaoh*, 23–24.

7. Benjamin Disraeli, *Contarini Fleming: A Psychological Romance*, 349–54; William Flavelle Monypenny and George Earle Buckle, *The Life of Benjamin Disraeli, Earl of Beaconsfield*, I, 136–80.

8. "Letters on Egypt, Edom, and the Holy Land," *AT* (August 18, 1838), 586–87; Alexander William Crawford Lindsay, *Letters on Egypt, Edom, and the Holy Land*, 147–48.

9. Hawkes, *The World of the Past*, I, 523; David Roberts, George Croby, and William Brockedon, *The Holy Land*, I, IV, V.

# CHAPTER VI

1. "Antiquarian Researches: Egyptian Antiquities," *GMHC*, Vol. IV (August, 1835), 187–88; Samuel Birch, "Description of an Egyptian Tomb Now Preserved in the British Museum," *AA*, Vol. XXIX (1842), 11; "Bunsen's Egypt," *BQR*, Vol. XXIII (April 1, 1856), 61; "The Egyptian Museum, Liverpool," *CEJ*, Vol. XVIII (September 18, 1852), 186; *The Georgian Era*, III, 61–62; Halls, *The Life of Henry Salt*, I, 91–191, 472–96, II, 3, 23–25, 40, 45, 192–93, 176–88; "Henry Salt," *GMHC*, Vol. XCVIII (April, 1828), 374; "Observations Relating to Some of the Antiquities of Egypt, from the Papers of the Late Mr. Davison," *QR*, Vol. XIX (July, 1818), 395; Salt, *Essay*; "Salt's Essay on Phonetic Hieroglyphics," *MR*, Vol. CVII (1825), 175–80.

2. Giovanni Belzoni, *Narrative of the Operations and Recent Discoveries Within the Pyramids, Temples, Tombs, and Excavations, in Egypt and Nubia*, I, 62–205, 318–33; II, 20–97, 46–135; "Captain the Honourable Charles L. Irby," *GMHC*, Vol. XXV (May, 1846), 536; Ceram, *The March of Archaeology*, 83; Maurice Willson Disher, *Pharaoh's Fool*, 67–73, 78–108, 112–32, 147–55; "Observations Relating to Some of the Antiquities of Egypt, from the Papers of the Late Mr. Davison, *QR*, Vol. XIX (July, 1818), 423; "The Story of Giovanni Belzoni," *HW*, Vol. II (March 1, 1851), 548–52; Wilson, *Signs & Wonders upon Pharaoh*, 27–28.

3. Ceram, *The March of Archaeology*, 78, 81, 135; "Mr. Joseph Bonomi," *AT* (March 9, 1878), 316; Victor Wolfgang Von Hagen, *Frederick Catherwood, Architect*, 10–17, 24–37, 167; Sir John Gardner Wilkinson, *Topography of Thebes*, 496; Wilson, *Signs & Wonders upon Pharaoh*, 32.

4. "Ancient Egyptians," *WR*, Vol. XXXVI (July, 1841), 13; Richard William Hamilton, "Address to the Royal Geographical Society of London," *JRGSL*, Vol. XII (1842), lxx–lxxi; Hawkes, *The World of the Past*, I, 561; Sir H. C. Rawlinson, "Address to the Royal Geographical Society," *JRGSL*,

Vol. XLVI (1876), cl–cli; Captain W. H. Smyth, "Address to the Royal Geographical Society," *JRGSL,* Vol. XX (1850), xxxviii; Von Hagen, *Frederick Catherwood,* 28; Sir John Gardner Wilkinson, *Manners and Customs of the Ancient Egyptians,* I, 12–15, 23, 212, 425; Sir John Gardner Wilkinson, "Notes on a Part of the Eastern Desert of Upper Egypt," *JRGSL,* Vol. XX (1850), 154–60; Sir John Gardner Wilkinson, "Wilkinson on Hieroglyphics," *FMTC,* Vol. II (October, 1830), 332–33; Wilson, *Signs & Wonders upon Pharaoh,* 31–32.

5. Ceram, *The March of Archaeology,* 78–79, 97–99.

6. Budge, *The Egyptian Sudan,* I, 55–61; Hawkes, *The World of the Past,* I, 452–59; "Travels in Ethiopia," *AQR,* Vol. XVIII (December, 1835), 423–40.

7. Ceram, *The March of Archaeology,* 105; George Ebers, *Richard Lepsius: A Biography* (trans. by Zoe Dona Underhill), 124–66; Fakhry, *The Pyramids,* 13; "The Great Pyramid," *NBR,* Vol. XLVII (September, 1867), 171–72; Richard Lepsius, *Letters from Egypt, Ethiopia, and the Peninsula of Sinai,* 12, 35, 45.

# CHAPTER VII

1. Belzoni, *Narrative,* I, 395–428; Ceram, *The March of Archaeology,* 84, 95–96; Cottrell, *The Mountains of Pharaoh,* 105–107; Disher, *Pharaoh's Fool,* 1–2, 108–11; Halls, *The Life of Henry Salt,* I, 60–61.

2. "Account of the Recent Discoveries in Egypt Respecting the Sphinx and the Great Pyramid," *EPJ,* Vol. I (1819), 90–96; Cottrell, *The Mountains of Pharaoh,* 95–108; Halls, *The Life of Henry Salt,* II, 65–90; "Observations Relating to Some of the Antiquities of Egypt, from the Papers of the Late Mr. Davison," *QR,* Vol. XIX (July, 1818), 395–419; Richard Howard Vyse, *Operations Carried on at the Pyramids of Gizeh in 1837,* II, 155–57.

3. Cottrell, *The Mountains of Pharaoh,* 98–132; Lindsay, *Letters on Egypt,* 155; "The Pyramids—Who Built Them?—And When?" *BEM,* Vol. XCIV (September, 1863), 356–57; Vyse, *Operations at Gizeh,* II, 155–57.

4. Samuel Birch, "Description of an Egyptian Tomb Now Preserved in the British Museum," *AA,* Vol. XXI (1842), 124; Cottrell, *The Mountains of Pharaoh,* 110–44; Fakhry, *The Pyramids,* 73, 93–94, 115, 127, 171; Barbara Mertz, *Temples, Tombs and Hieroglyphs: The Story of Egyptology,* 83; J. S. Perring, "On the Construction of the Pyramids," *AT* (June 15, 1844), 549–59.

5. "Recent Discoveries in the Great Pyramid of Egypt—Ancient Egyptian Weight," *Nature,* Vol. VII (December 26, 1872), 146–47.

6. George Stanley Faber, *A Dissertation on the Mysteries of the Cabyri;* George Stanley Faber, *The Origin of Pagan Idolatry;* "Mr. Faber on the

Pyramid of Cephrenes, Lately Opened by Belzone," *BEM*, Vol. V (August, 1819), 582–85; "Reverend George Stanley Faber, B.D.," *GMHC*, Vol. XLI (May, 1854), 537–39.

7. Hermogenes, "The Pyramids: Chapter I, Interior Mathematical Characters," *FMTC*, Vol. XVI (October, 1837), 402–10; Hermogenes, "The Pyramids: Chapter II, Exterior Mathematical Characters," *FMTC*, Vol. XVI (November, 1837), 627–36; Hermogenes, "The Pyramids: Chapter III, Their Builders and Historical Epochs," *FMTC*, Vol. XVI (December, 1837), 736–47.

8. The material on Wilson, Taylor, and Smyth is taken from the following works: George W. Anderson, "The Great Pyramid of Gizeh," *BQ* (April, 1869), 195–209; Edmund Blunden, *Keats's Publisher: A Memoir of John Taylor (1781–1864)*, 225–28; Cottrell, *The Mountains of Pharaoh*, 157–67; Martin Gardner, *Fads and Fallacies in the Name of Science*, 130–82; "The Great Pyramid," *NBR*, Vol. XLVII (September, 1867), 149–82; "History and Biography," *WR*, Vol. XXXII (July, 1967), 293–95; "Miscellanea," *AT* (May 27, 1865), 725; Richard A. Proctor, "The Religion of the Great Pyramid," *FMTC*, Vol. XV (March, 1877), 331; Charles Piazzi Smyth, "Notes from the Great Pyramid," *AT* (February 25, 1865), 275; John Wilson, *The Lost Solar System of the Ancients Discovered*, I, 181–351, II, 179–232.

9. Richard A. Proctor, "The Mystery of the Pyramids," *BEL*, Vol. XXII (1877), 434–52; Richard A. Proctor, "The Problem of the Great Pyramid," *CR*, Vol. XXXVI (September, 1879), 94–119; Proctor, "The Religion of the Great Pyramid," *FMTC*, Vol. XV (March, 1877), 332–43.

10. Information about nineteenth-century interest in Egyptian obelisks can be found in the following works: Belzoni, *Narrative*, II, 99–123; Budge, *The Rosetta Stone*, 202–203; "Cory's Ancient Fragments, &c.," *BEM*, Vol. XLIV (October, 1838), 110; Disher, *Pharaoh's Fool*, 136–48; Evans, *A History of the Society of Antiquaries*, 330–31; Hermogenes, "Dr. Young and Mrs. Belzoni," *FMTC*, Vol. IX (June, 1834), 636; "The History of Egypt," *PR*, Vol. II. (1846), 14; James King, *Cleopatra's Needle*, 25–26, 36–57; Baron Samuel Selig de Kusel, *An Englishman's Recollections of Egypt*, 103–104; "Marquis Spineto on Hieroglyphics," *BEM*, Vol. XXIV (September, 1828), 323; Salt, *Essay*, v–vii; Bayle St. John, "The Old Egyptian Monuments," *AT* (November 20, 1852), 1271; Bayle St. John, "State of Egyptian Monuments," *AT* (April 12, 1851), 406–407; "Wall on Egyptian Hieroglyphics, and on the Origin of Alphabetic Writing," *ERCJ*, Vol. LXIV (October, 1836), 46; Sir J. Gardner Wilkinson, "Wilkinson on Hieroglyphics," *FMTC*, Vol. II (October, 1830), 332; "William John Bankes, Esq.," *GMHC*, Vol. XLIV, n.s. (August, 1855), 205; Wilson, *Cleopatra's Needle*, 17–18, 119–200; Wilson, *Signs & Wonders upon Pharaoh*, 18, 29–30.

11. Baikie, *A Century of Excavation*, 18–34; Wilson, *Signs & Wonders upon Pharaoh*, 46–48, 69–72.

## CHAPTER VIII

1. Edward Frederic Benson, *King Edward VII: An Appreciation*, 48–49; "Fine-Art Gossip," AT (March 12, 1870), 364; Henry Richard Whates, *The Life and Times of King Edward VII*, II, 33–40; Sir John Gardner Wilkinson, "The Prince's Visit to Egypt," AT (June 5, 1869), 764; Wilson, *Signs & Wonders upon Pharaoh*, 52–53.

2. J. Lewis Farley, "Wintering in Egypt," BEL, Vol. XX (March, 1873), 70–71; "Our Weekly Gossip," AT (April 18, 1863), 526.

3. Wilson, *Signs & Wonders upon Pharaoh*, 99–101.

4. Andrew Leith Adams, *Notes of a Naturalist in the Nile Valley and Malta*, 1–2, 20–21, 31–32, 38–45, 56–58; King, *Cleopatra's Needle*, 14; Alexander Henry Rhind, "One of the Simple Forms of Burial in Use Among the Ancient Egyptians, Observed in a Recent Excavation at Geezeh," PSAS, Vol. II (1859), 274–76; Alexander Henry Rhind, *Thebes: Its Tombs and Their Tenants Ancient and Present, Including a Record of Excavations in the Necropolis*, 75–84, 87–111, 118–74; John Stuart, *Memoir of the Late Alexander Henry Rhind*, with Vol. V of PSAS (1865), 1–3, 6–9, 11–27, 30–43.

5. "Bunsen's *Egypt* and the Chronology of the Bible," QR, Vol. CV (April, 1859), 418–21; Leonard Horner, "An Account of Some Recent Research near Cairo," PTRSL (1855), 106–109, 113, 119–21, 123–33; Leonard Horner, "An Account of Some Recent Researches near Cairo," PTRSL (1858), 53–63, 75–76.

6. M. E. Grant Duff, "Egypt," CR, Vol. XXIII (February, 1874), 406–408, 411, 420–36; Daniel, *The Idea of Prehistory*, 14, 58–59; Sir John Lubbock, "Notes on the Discovery of Stone Implements in Egypt," JAI, Vol. IV (1875), 215–22.

7. A. J. Jukes Browne, "On Some Flint Implements from Egypt," JAI, Vol. VII (1878), 396–412. For an account of modern-day discoveries at Helwan, see Zaki Y. Saad, *The Excavations at Helwan: Art and Civilization in the First and Second Egyptian Dynasties* (ed. by J. Frank Autry), Norman, 1969.

8. Richard Francis Burton, "Stones and Bones from Egypt and Midian," JAI, Vol. VIII (1879), 290–318.

## CHAPTER IX

1. George Rawlinson, *A History of Ancient Egypt*, in *The Works of George Rawlinson*, II, 133.

2. "Antiquarian Researches: Egyptian Antiquities," GMHC, Vol. IV (August, 1835), 188–89; "British Archaeological Association: First An-

nual Meeting, Canterbury, September, 1844," *AJ* (1846), 267–82; C. W. C., "Chronology of Egyptian History," *WR*, Vol. XLIII (March–June, 1845), 104, 143; John Davidson, "Extracts from the Correspondence of the Late Mr. Davidson, During his Residence in Moscow," *JRGSL*, Vol. VI (1836), 430–33; Warren Royal Dawson, "Pettigrew's Demonstrations upon Mummies: A Chapter in the History of Egyptology," *JEA*, Vol. XX (1934), 170–72; "Egyptian Mummies," *AQR*, Vol. XVIII (September, 1835), 172; Augustus Bozzi Granville, "An Essay on Egyptian Mummies: With Observations on the Art of Embalming Among the Ancient Egyptians," *PTRSL* (1925), 269–316; "On Superstitions Connected with the History and Practice of Medicine and Surgery," *AT* (February 3, 1844), 107–109; Thomas Joseph Pettigrew, "Account of the Examination of the Mummy of Pet-Mantioh-Mes," *AA*, Vol. XXVII (1838), 262–73; "Unrolling a Mummy," *AT* (July 20, 1833), 481–83.

3. Warren Royal Dawson, "Anatasi, Sallier, and Harris and Their Papyri," *JEA*, Vol. XXXV (December, 1949), 162; Sir William Drummond, *Origines: Or Remarks on the Origin of Several Empires, States and Cities*; "Egyptian Antiquities," *NAR*, Vol. LXV (October, 1829), 369–84; Anthony Charles Harris, *Hieroglyphical Standards Supposed to Be the Nomes or Toparchies*; "Hieroglyphics," *ERCJ*, Vol. XLV (December, 1826), 96; "Our Library Table," *AT* (June 24, 1843), 558; William Palmer, *Egyptian Chronicles, with a Harmony of Sacred and Egyptian Chronology, and an Appendix of Babylonian and Assyrian Antiquities*; James Prichard, *An Analysis of Egyptian Mythology;* "Recent Works on Egyptology," *NAR*, Vol. XCVI (January, 1863), 111–12; George Henry Wathen, *Arts, Antiquities and Chronology of Ancient Egypt.*

4. "Isaac Cullimore," *GMHC*, Vol. XXVIII (August, 1852), 208; William Hayes Word, "The Babylonian Seals," *SM*, Vol. I (January, 1887), 81.

5. "Obituary Dr. S. Birch," *AC*, Vol. XXIX (January 2, 1886), 10; "Dr. Samuel Birch," *AT* (January 2, 1886), 34–35.

6. Edward Hincks, "On the Age of the Eighteenth Dynasty of Manetho," *TRIA*, Vol. XXI (1846), 5; Edward Hincks, "On the Defacement of Divine and Royal Names on Egyptian Monuments," *TRIA*, Vol. XXI (1848), 107–11; "Our Library Table," *AT* (May 11, 1844), 427.

7. Samuel Birch, ed. *Records of the Past*, II, 101–102; Harvey Carlisle, "Mr. Charles Wycliffe Goodwin," *AT* (March 23, 1878), 379–80; Charles Wycliffe Goodwin, "Hieratic Papyri," *CE* (1858), 226–82; Charles Wycliffe Goodwin, "The Story of Saneha: An Egyptian Tale of Four Thousand Years Ago," *FMTC*, Vol. LXXI (February, 1865), 187–202; "Our Weekly Gossip," *AT* (February 2, 1861), 159.

8. "Ancient Egypt Under the Pharaohs," *BQR*, Vol. XIII (February, May, 1851), 93–124; "Ancient Egypt Under the Pharaohs," *PR*, Vol. VII (1851), 2–3, 19–24; Henry Brugsch-Bey, *A History of Egypt Under the Pharaohs Derived Entirely from the Monuments* (trans. by Phillip Smith);

"Brugsch's *Egypt Under the Pharaohs*," *ERCJ*, Vol. CLC (July, 1879), 77–115; "Brugsch's History of Egypt," *QR*, Vol. CXLVII (April, 1879), 431–32; "Bunsen's *Egypt*," *BQR*, Vol. CV (April, 1859), 382–85; C. W. C., "Chronology of Egyptian History," *WR*, Vol. XLIII (March–June, 1845), 142; "The Definite Results of Egyptology," *N*, Vol. VC (July 4, 1867), 5; "Egypt Under the Pharaohs," *BQR*, Vol. XIII (February, 1851), 97–122; "Egyptology and the Two Exodes," *BQR*, Vol. XXXII (October, 1860), 443–46; Evans, *A History of the Society of Antiquaries*, 275; Hermogenes, "The Pyramids," *FMTC*, Vol. XVI (December, 1837), 747; "The History of Egypt," *PR*, Vol. II (1846), 2–31; "The New Pharonic Tablets of Memphis and Abydos," *BQR*, Vol. XLI (January, 1856), 189–90; "Our Weekly Gossip," *AT* (February 1, 1862), 157; Thomas George Peabody, "The First Glimpse of Historical Religion," *URRM*, Vol. XII (December, 1879), 581–82; Rawlinson, *A History of Ancient Egypt*, II, 110–11, 132–34, 180–82; "Rudiments of a Vocabulary of Egyptian Hieroglyphics," *AT* (November 3, 1838), 788–89; "Sharpe's History of Egypt," *ERCJ*, Vol. LXXXVIII (July, 1848), 32–40; Samuel Sharpe, *The History of Egypt from the Earliest Times Till the Conquest by the Arabs A.D. 640*, I, 22–52.

9. C. Pickering Clarke, Stanley Lane-Pool, et al., *Picturesque Palestine, Sinai and Egypt* (ed. by Sir Charles W. Wilson), IV, 125, 129–34.

10. Gustave Doré, *The Doré Bible Gallery*, 17–19; William Smith, *The Illustrated History of the Bible*, 87–110.

11. "The Monumental History of Egypt," *AT* (1854), 1421–23; Henry G. Tomkins, *The Life and Times of Joseph in the Light of Egyptian Lore*, Vol. XVII of *By-Paths of Bible Knowledge*, 320.

12. Disher, *Pharaoh's Fool*, 32–43, 48, 158–64; "The Egyptian Museum, Liverpool," *CEJ*, Vol. XVIII (September 18, 1852), 184–86; Von Hagen, *Frederick Catherwood*, 38–42.

13. "The Pyramid Cemetery," *PM*, Vol. III (October 4, 1834), 389–90.

14. Dawson, "Pettigrew's Demonstrations upon Mummies: A Chapter in the History of Egyptology," *JEA*, Vol. XX (1934), 170–82.

15. Blunden, *Keats's Publisher*, 225; Morton Norton Cohen, *Rider Haggard: His Life and Works*, 120–21, 239, 274, 308–309; George Gordon, Lord Byron, *The Poetical Works of Lord Byron* (ed. by Thomas More et al.), 610; Sir Henry Rider Haggard, *The Days of My Life: An Autobiography* (ed. by C. J. Longman), 30–38, 155–58, 254–63; "New Books and Reprints," *TLS* (April 30, 1925), 301; "Novels of the Week," *AT* (June 16, 1877), 767.

# CHAPTER X

1. "Amelia B. Edwards," *Critic*, Vol. XX (April 23, 1892), 241; Matilda Barbara Betham-Edwards, "Amelia B. Edwards: Her Childhood and Early

Life," *NEM*, Vol. VII (January, 1893), 549–50, 553, 555–56; Matilda Barbara Betham-Edwards, *Mid-Victorian Memories*, 111, 114; Amelia B. Edwards, *Untrodden Peaks and Unfrequented Valleys*; Sallie Joy White, "Amelia B. Edwards," *NEM*, Vol. II (April, 1890), 194–98.

2. "Amelia B. Edwards," *Critic*, Vol. XX (April 23, 1892), 241; Amelia B. Edwards, *A Thousand Miles up the Nile*; "A Thousand Miles up the Nile," *AT* (February 17, 1877), 219–20.

3. Amelia B. Edwards, *Pharaohs, Fellahs and Explorers*, 40–41; "Ancient Monuments of Egypt," *London Times* (November 27, 1880), 10; "Egyptian Antiquities," *London Times* (March 30, 1882), 8; Canon Rawlinson, "On the Supposed Antiquity of Civilization in Egypt," *LH* (1876), 101; "The Story-City of Pithom and the Route of the Exodus," *AT* (March 14, 1885), 350.

4. "Amelia B. Edwards," *Critic*, Vol. XX (April 23, 1892), 245; William C. Winslow, "The Egypt Exploration Fund in the United States," *AC*, Vol. XXVII (May 2, 1885), 319.

5. "Amelia Blanford Edwards," *LLA*, Vol. XXXIX (July 2, 1892), 64; Amelia B. Edwards, "My Home Life," *Arena*, Vol. XIX (June, 1891), 300–10; "From West to East," *AM*, Vol. LXIX (May, 1892), 682–84; "Miss Edwards' Pharaohs, Fellahs and Explorers," *Critic*, Vol. XX (January 2, 1891), 2–3; "Pharaohs, Fellahs, and Explorers," *AT* (February 27, 1892), 274.

6. James Henry Breasted, *A History of Egypt*, 442, 447; Edwards, *Pharaohs, Fellahs, and Explorers*, 41–42; Amelia B. Edwards, "The Site of Raamses," *AC*, Vol. XVII (April 24, 1880), 307–308; Gardiner, *Egypt of the Pharaohs*, 461; C. R. Gillett, "Pithom-Heroapolis-Succoth," *AR*, Vol. VIII (July, 1887), 84; Stanley Lane-Poole, "The Excavations at Pithom," *AT* (April 7, 1883), 450; Sir Gaston Maspero, *History of Egypt, Chaldea, Syria, Babylonia, and Assyria* (trans. by M. L. McClure), V, 270; Édouard Naville, *The Story-City of Pithom and the Route of the Exodus*, 1–3; Reginald Stuart Poole, "The Progress of Discovery in Egypt," *AC*, Vol. XXIII (February 24, 1883), 140, Vol. XXIII (April 7, 1883), 246; "The Story-City of Pithom and the Route of the Exodus," *AT* (March 14, 1885), 350–51.

# CHAPTER XI

1. Ceram, *The March of Archaeology*, 104; Cottrell, *The Mountains of Pharaoh*, 204; Daniel, *A Hundred Years of Archaeology*, 175–76, 204; Daniel, *The Idea of Prehistory*, 69, 88–89; Hawkes, *The World of the Past*, I, 52; "Methods and Aims in Archaeology," *N*, Vol. LXXIX (September 15, 1904), 224–25; Percy E. Newberry, "William Matthew Flinders Petrie," *JEA*, Vol. XXIX (December, 1943), 69–70.

L

2. Cottrell, *The Mountains of Pharaoh*, 168–70; Stephen B. Luce, "Archaeological News and Discussions," *AJA*, Vol. XLVI (October–December, 1942), 546.

3. Cottrell, *The Mountains of Pharaoh*, 168–71; Newberry, "William Matthew Flinders Petrie," *JEA*, Vol. XXIX (December, 1943), 68.

4. Cottrell, *The Mountains of Pharaoh*, 168–71, 175–76, 223; Daniel, *A Hundred Years of Archaeology*, 174–75; Amelia B. Edwards, "The Pyramids and Temples of Gizeh," *AC*, Vol. XXIV (November 10, 1883), 309; Newberry, "William Matthew Flinders Petrie," *JEA*, Vol. XXIX (December, 1943), 68; Sir William Matthew Flinders Petrie, "Excavations at the Pyramids," *AC*, Vol. XX (December 17, 1881), 462; Sir William Matthew Flinders Petrie, *The Pyramids and Temples of Gizeh*, 24, 51–58, 63–67, 74–76; "The Pyramids," *SR*, Vol. LVI (September 9, 1883), 405; "Recent Pyramid Work," *CJPLSA*, Vol. II (July 15, 1885), 454–56.

5. Breasted, *A History of Egypt*, 442; Edwards, *Pharaohs, Fellahs, and Explorers*, 50–52, 54, 57; Sir William Matthew Flinders Petrie, *Tanis Part I, 1883–4: Second Memoir of the Egypt Exploration Fund*, 2–3, 22–24.

6. Edwards, *Pharaohs, Fellahs, and Explorers*, 179–81; Ernest Arthur Gardner and Francis Llewellyn Griffith, *Naukratis: Part II*, 4–11; Michaelis, *A Century of Archaeological Discoveries*, 261; "Naukratis and the Greeks in Ancient Egypt," *QR*, Vol. CLXIV (January, 1887), 63, 78–86; Sir William Matthew Flinders Petrie, Alexander Stuart Murray, and Francis Llewellyn Griffith, *Tanis Part II: Nebesheh (Am) and Defenneh (Tahpanhes)*, 47; Reginald Stuart Poole, "Egypt Exploration Fund," *AC*, Vol. XXVII (January 3, 1885), 17, Vol. XXVII (May 30, 1885), 391.

7. Edwards, *Pharaohs, Fellahs, and Explorers*, 48–69; Petrie, Murray and Griffith, *Tanis Part II*, 47–51.

8. Edwards, *Pharaohs, Fellahs, and Explorers*, 76–77; Hawkes, *The World of the Past*, I, 52; Michaelis, *A Century of Archaeological Discoveries*, 261.

9. C. W. Ceram (Kurt W. Marek), *Gods, Graves, and Scholars: The Story of Archaeology* (trans. by E. B. Garside), 149–53; Cottrell, *The Mountains of Pharaoh*, 186–96.

10. Cottrell, *The Mountains of Pharaoh*, 213–14; Daniel, *A Hundred Years of Archaeology*, 176–77; Alan H. Gardiner, "Sir William Flinders Petrie," *Nature*, Vol. CL (August 15, 1942), 204; Hawkes, *The World of the Past*, I, 52; Sir William Matthew Flinders Petrie, "Archaeology in the Past Century," *SAS*, Vol. LI (January 26, 1901), 209–60; Sir William Matthew Flinders Petrie, "Recent Research in Egypt," *ARRSI* (July, 1897), 571–73; Sir William Matthew Flinders Petrie, "Recent Years of Egyptian Exploration," *APSM*, Vol. LVI (April, 1900), 627–30.

11. Cottrell, *The Mountains of Pharaoh*, 213–14; Daniel, *A Hundred Years of Archaeology*, 176–77; Hawkes, *The World of the Past*, I, 52; Sir

William Matthew Flinders Petrie, "Egypt and Israel," *CR*, Vol. LII (August, 1896), 500–503; Petrie, "Recent Research in Egypt," *ARRSI* (July, 1897), 573; Petrie, "Recent Years of Egyptian Exploration," *APSM*, Vol. LVI (April, 1900), 627–30.

12. Cottrell, *The Mountains of Pharaoh*, 197–98; Newberry, "William Matthew Flinders Petrie," *JEA*, Vol. XXIX (December, 1943), 69; Petrie, "Recent Research in Egypt," *ARRSI* (July, 1897), 572; Petrie, "Recent Years of Egyptian Exploration," *APSM*, Vol. LVI (April, 1900), 628; Sir William Matthew Flinders Petrie, "The Royal Tombs at Abydos: An Account of Recent Discoveries," *HMM*, Vol. CIII (October, 1901), 682–87; Sir William Matthew Flinders Petrie and Francis Llewellyn Griffith, *The Royal Tombs of the Earliest Dynasties 1901: Part II*, 5–9; Sir William Matthew Flinders Petrie, "The Ten Temples of Abydos," *HMM*, Vol. CVII (November, 1903), 334–40; H. D. Rawnsley, "With the Predynastic Kings and the Kings of the First Three Dynasties at Abydos," *AM*, Vol. XCI (February, 1903), 221–22, 227.

# Bibliography

## I. PRIMARY SOURCES

### A. BOOKS

Adams, Andrew Leith. *Notes of a Naturalist in the Nile Valley and Malta.* Edinburgh, 1870.

Ammianus Marcellinus. *The Roman Historie.* Trans. by Philemon Holland. London, 1909.

Apuleius. *The Golden Ass of Apuleius.* Trans. by William Adlington, ed. by Charles Whibley. London, 1893.

Ausonius. *Ausonius.* Trans. by H. G. Evelyn White. 2 vols. London, 1919.

Bacon, Sir Francis. *The Works of Francis Bacon.* Ed. by James Spedding, Robert Leslie Ellis, and Douglas Denon Heath. 15 vols. Boston, 1862.

Belzoni, Giovanni. *Narrative of the Operations and Recent Discoveries Within the Pyramids, Temples, Tombs, and Excavations, in Egypt and Nubia.* 2 vols. London, 1822.

Benjamin of Tudela. *Peregrination, in Purchas His Pilgrimes.* Ed. by Samuel Purchas. Vol. VIII. Glasgow, 1905.

Berkeley, Sir William. *The Lost Lady.* Vol. XII, pp. 537–68, in *A Select Collection of Old English Plays.* Ed. by W. Carew Hazlitt. 15 vols. London, 1875.

Betham-Edwards, Matilda Barbara. *Mid-Victorian Memories.* New York, 1919.

Birch, Samuel, ed. *Records of the Past.* 12 vols. London, 1874–81.

Bovet, Richard. *Pandaemonium, or, The Devil's Cloyster.* Ed. by Montague Summers. Aldington, 1951.

Boyle, Robert. *The Works of the Honourable Robert Boyle.* 6 vols. London, 1772.

Browne, Sir Thomas. *The Works of Sir Thomas Browne.* Ed. by Charles Sayle. 3 vols. Edinburgh, 1927.

Browne, William George. *Travels in Africa, Egypt, and Syria from the Year 1792 to 1798.* London, 1806.

Bruce, James. *Travels to Discover the Source of the Nile in the Years 1768, 1769, 1770, 1771, 1772, and 1773.* 5 vols. Edinburgh, 1790.

Brugsch-Bey, Henry. *A History of Egypt Under the Pharaohs Derived Entirely from the Monuments.* Trans. by Phillip Smith. 2 vols. London, 1881.

Byron, George Gordon, Sixth Baron. *The Poetical Works of Lord Byron.* Ed. by Thomas More et al. London, 1837.

Caxton, William. *Caxton's Mirrour of the World.* Ed. by Oliver H. Prior. London, 1913.

Clarke, C. Pickering, Stanley Lane-Poole, et al. *Picturesque Palestine, Sinai and Egypt.* Ed. by Sir Charles W. Wilson. 4 vols. London, 1881–84.

Clarke, Edward Daniel. *The Tomb of Alexander.* Cambridge, 1805.

———. *Travels in Various Countries of Europe, Asia and Africa.* 6 vols. Cambridge, 1810–23.

Clayton, Robert. *A Journal from Grand Cairo to Mount Sinai, and Back Again: To Which Are Added Remarks on the Origin of Hieroglyphics.* London, 1753.

Coates, Henry. *The British Don Juan.* London, 1823.

Collins, Francis. *Voyages to Portugal, Spain, Sicily, Malta, Asia-Minor, Egypt, &c. &c. from 1796 to 1801.* London, 1822.

Colonna, Francesco. *The Strife of Love in a Dream; Being the Elizabethan Version of the First Book of the Hypnerotomachia of Francesco Colonna.* Ed. by Andrew Lang. London, 1890.

Conder, Joseph. *Egypt, Nubia, and Abyssinia.* In Vols. I and II of *The Modern Traveller.* London, 1827.

Coventry, Henry. *Philemon to Hydaspes: Or, The History of False Religion in the Earlier Pagan World.* Glasgow, 1761.

Dalton, Richard. *Remarks on Prints Intended to Be Published, Relative to the Manners, Customs, &c. of the Present Inhabitants of Egypt: From Drawings Made on the Spot, A.D. 1749.* London, 1781.

Dekker, Thomas. *Newes from Graves-end.* In *The Plague Pamphlets of Thomas Dekker.* Ed. by F. P. Wilson. Oxford, 1925.

Deverell, Robert. *Andalusia; Or, Notes Tending to Show That the Yellow Fever of the West Indies, and of Andalusia in Spain, Was a Disease Well Known to the Ancients.* London, 1805.

————. *A Supplement to Notes on the Ancient Method of Treating the Fever of Andalusia, Now Called the Yellow Fever; Deduced from an Explanation of the Hieroglyphics Painted upon the Cambridge Mummy.* London, 1806.

Diodorus Siculus. *Diodorus of Sicily.* Trans. by Russel M. Geer. 12 vols. In *The Loeb Classical Library.* Ed. by E. Capps, W. H. D. Rouse, L. A. Post, and E. H. Warmington. London, 1954.

Disraeli, Benjamin. *Contarini Fleming: A Psychological Romance.* London, 1927.

Doré, Gustave. *The Doré Bible Gallery.* Philadelphia, 1890.

Drummond, Sir William. *Memoir on the Antiquity of the Zodiacs of Esneh and Dendera.* London, 1821.

————. *Origines: Or Remarks on the Origin of Several Empires, States and Cities.* 4 vols. London, 1829.

Ebers, Georg. *Arachne: A Historical Romance.* Trans. by Mary J. Safford. New York, 1898.

————. *The Bride of the Nile: A Romance.* Trans. by Clara Bell. New York, 1887.

————. *An Egyptian Princess.* Trans. by Eleanor Grove. 2 vols. New York, 1890.

————. *The Emperor: A Romance.* Trans. by Clara Bell. 2 vols. New York, 1889.

————. *Homo Sum: A Novel.* Trans. by Clara Bell. New York, 1890.

——. *Joshua: A Story of Biblical Times*. Trans. by Mary J. Safford. New York, 1890.

——. *A Question: The Idyl of a Picture by His Friend Alma Tadema Related by George Ebers*. Trans. by Mary J. Safford. New York, 1890.

——. *Serapis: A Romance*. Trans. by Clara Bell. New York, 1889.

——. *The Sisters: A Romance*. Trans. by Clara Bell. New York, 1891.

——. *Uarda: A Romance of Ancient Egypt*. Trans. by Clara Bell. New York, 1884, reprinted in 1890.

——. *A Word Only a Word*. Trans. by Mary J. Safford. New York, 1890.

Eden, Frederic. *The Nile Without a Dragoman*. London, 1871.

Edwards, Amelia Blanford. *Pharaoh, Fellahs, and Explorers*. New York, 1901.

——. *A Thousand Miles up the Nile*. New York, 1889, London, 1890.

——. *Untrodden Peaks and Unfrequented Valleys*. Leipzig, 1873.

Evelyn, John. *Memoirs of John Evelyn, Esq*. Ed. by William Bray. 5 vols. London, 1827.

Faber, George Stanley. *A Dissertation on the Mysteries of the Cabyri*. 2 vols. London, 1803.

——. *The Origin of Pagan Idolatry*. 3 vols. London, 1816.

Freeman, Joseph J. *A Tour in South Africa*. London, 1851.

Fuller, Thomas. *A Pisgah-Sight of Palestine*. London, 1650.

Gardner, Ernest Arthur, and Francis Llewellyn Griffith. *Naukratis: Part II*. London, 1888.

Gaule, John. *Select Cases of Conscience Touching Witches and Witchcrafts*. London, 1646.

Gibbon, Edward. *The History of the Decline and Fall of the Roman Empire*. 12 vols. London, 1807.

Glanvil, Joseph. *Saducismus Triumphatus: Or Full and Plain Evidence Concerning Witches and Apparitions*. London, 1688.

Godwyn, Thomas. *Moses and Aaron. Civil and Ecclesiastical Rites, Used by the Ancient Hebrewes. Herein Likewise Is*

*Shewed What Customes the Hebrews Borrowed from Heathen People: And That Many Heathenish Customs, Originally Have Beene Unwarrantable Imitations of the Hebrews*. London, 1626.

Greaves, John. *Pyramidographia: Or a Description of the Pyramids in Egypt*. London, 1646.

Greenhill, Thomas. *Nepoxnoeia: Or the Art of Embalming*. London, 1705.

Guthrie, William. *A General History of the World*. 13 vols. London, 1764–67.

Haggard, Sir Henry Rider. *The Days of My Life: An Autobiography*. Ed. by C. J. Longman. 2 vols. London, 1926.

Hakluyt, Richard, ed. *The Principal Navigations, Voyages, Traffiques & Discoveries of the English Nation*. 11 vols. Glasgow, 1904.

Halls, John James. *The Life and Correspondence of Henry Salt, Esq*. 2 vols. London, 1834.

Harff, Arnold Von. *The Pilgrimage of Arnold Von Harff Knight*. Trans. by Malcolm Letts, in *Works Issued By The Hakluyt Society*. 2d ser., No. XCIV. London, 1946.

*The Harleian Miscellany: Or, A Collection of Scarce, Curious and Entertaining Pamphlets and Tracts*. 12 vols. London, 1811.

Harris, Anthony Charles. *Hieroglyphical Standards Supposed to Be the Nomes or Toparchies*. London, 1852.

Hawkes, Jacquetta, ed. *The World of the Past*. 2 vols. New York, 1963.

Hermes Mercurius Trismegistus. *The Divine Pymander of Hermes Mercurius Trismegistus*. Trans. by John Everard. London, 1613.

Herodotus. *The Famous Hystory of Herodotus*. Trans. by B. R. In *The Tudor Translations Second Series*. Ed. by Charles Whibley. New York, 1924.

———. *Herodotus*. Trans. by J. Enoch Powell. 2 vols. Oxford, 1949.

Heylin, Peter. *Microcosmus: Or a Little Description of the Great World*. Oxford, 1621.

Heywood, Thomas. *The English Traveller*. London, 1633.

Holland, Henry. *A Treatise Against Witchcraft*. Cambridge, 1590.

Homes, Nathanael. *Daemonologie, and Theologie*. London, 1650.

Irwin, Eyles. *Eastern Eclogues Written During a Tour Through Arabia, Egypt, and Other Parts of Asia and Africa*. London, 1780.

————. *Occasional Epistles Written During a Journey from London to Busrah in the Gulf of Persia*. London, 1783.

Jackson, John. *Chronological Antiquities: Or, The Antiquities and Chronology of the Most Ancient Kingdoms*. 3 vols. London, 1752.

James I. *King James the First: Daemonologie (1597): News from Scotland (1591)*. Intro. by G. B. Harrison. New York, 1924.

Jonson, Ben. *The Alchemist*. Ed. by Charles Montgomery Hathaway. In *Yale Studies In English*. Ed. by Albert S. Cook. New York, 1903.

Josephus, Flavius. *The Works of Flavius Josephus*. Trans. by William Whiston. New York, 1887.

Knolles, Richard. *The Generall Historie of the Turkes*. London, 1610.

Knox, John. *A New Collection of Voyages, Discoveries and Travels*. London, 1767.

Kusel, Baron Samuel Selig de. *An Englishman's Recollections of Egypt*. London, 1915.

Laertius, Diogenes. *Lives of Eminent Philosophers*. Trans. by R. D. Hicks. 2 vols. London, 1952.

Legh, Thomas. *Narrative of a Journey in Egypt and the Country Beyond the Cataracts*. London, 1816.

Leo, Africanus. *The History and Description of Africa*. Trans. by John Pory, ed. by Robert Brown. Vols. 92–94 of *Works Issued by the Hakluyt Society*. 1st ser. New York, 1963.

Lepsius, Richard. *Letters from Egypt, Ethiopia, and the Peninsula of Sinai*. London, 1853.

Lewis, Sir George Cornewall. *An Historicall Survey of the Astronomy of the Ancients*. London, 1862.

Lindsay, Alexander William Crawford, Twenty-fifth Earl of

Crawford and Eighth Earl of Balcarres. *Letters on Egypt, Edom, and the Holy Land.* London, 1858.

Lithgow, William. *The Totall Discourse of the Rare Adventures & Painefull Peregrinations of Long Nineteene Yeares Travayles.* Glasgow, 1906.

Long, George, and Henry Ellis. *The British Museum Egyptian Antiquities.* In *The Library of Entertaining Knowledge.* 2 vols. London, 1883.

Lowellin, David. *The Admirable Travels of Misseurs Thomas Jenkins and David Lowellin Through the Unknown Tracts of Africa.* Dublin, 1792.

Madden, Richard Robert. *Memoirs of Dr. Madden.* Ed. by Thomas More Madden. New York, 1892.

Mandeville, Sir John. *Mandeville's Travels.* Ed. by P. Hamelius. 2 vols. London, 1919.

Marlowe, Christopher. *The Complete Plays of Christopher Marlowe.* Ed. by Irving Ribner. New York, 1963.

Marston, John. *The Works of John Marston.* Ed. by A. H. Bullen. 3 vols. London, 1832.

Massinger, Philip. *The Plays of Philip Massinger.* 4 vols. London, 1805.

Maundrell, Henry. *A Journey from Aleppo to Jerusalem at Easter, A.D. 1697.* In *Early Travels in Palestine.* Ed. by Thomas Wright. London, 1848.

Mavor, William, ed. *Historical Account of the Most Celebrated Voyages, Travels, and Discoveries.* 25 vols. London, 1801.

———. *Universal History, Ancient and Modern.* 25 vols. London, 1802.

Montagu, John, Fourth Earl of Sandwich. *A Voyage Performed by the Late Earl of Sandwich in the Years 1738 and 1739.* London, 1799.

Monypenny, William Flavelle, and George Earle Buckle. *The Life of Benjamin Disraeli, Earl of Beaconsfield.* 6 vols. London, 1910.

Mure, William. *Brief Remarks on the Chronology of the Egyptian Dynasties.* London, 1829.

Naville, Édouard. *The Store-City of Pithom and the Route of the Exodus.* London, 1888.

Newton, Sir Isaac. *The Chronology of Ancient Kingdoms Amended.* London, 1728.

Nichols, John. *Literary Anecdotes of the Eighteenth Century.* 9 vols. London, 1812–15.

Norden, Frederick Lewis. *Travels in Egypt and Nubia.* 2 vols. London, 1757.

Osburn, William. *Israel in Egypt, or the Books of Genesis and Exodus. Illustrated by Existing Monuments.* London, 1854.

Otter, William. *The Life and Remains of the Reverend Edward Daniel Clarke.* London, 1824.

Palmer, William. *Egyptian Chronicles, with a Harmony of Sacred and Egyptian Chronology, and an Appendix of Babylonian and Assyrian Antiquities.* London, 1863.

Pausanias. *The Description of Greece by Pausanias Translated from the Greek.* 3 vols. London, 1824.

Perrot, George, and Charles Chipiez. *A History of Art in Ancient Egypt.* Trans. by Walter Armstrong. 2 vols. London, 1883.

Perry, Charles. *A View of the Levant.* London, 1743.

Petrie, Sir William Matthew Flinders. *The Pyramids and Temples of Gizeh.* London, 1885.

———. *The Royal Tombs of the First Dynasty 1900: Part I.* London, 1900.

———. *Tanis Part I, 1883–4: Second Memoir of the Egypt Exploration Fund.* London, 1889.

———, Alexander Stuart Murray, and Francis Llewellyn Griffith. *Tanis Part II, Nebesheh (Am) And Defenneh (Tahpanhes).* London, 1888.

——— and Arthur Edward Pearse Brome Weigall. *Abydos Part I: 1902.* London, 1902.

——— and Francis Llewellyn Griffith. *The Royal Tombs of the Earliest Dynasties 1901: Part II.* London, 1901.

———, Cecil Smith, Ernest Gardner, and Barclay V. Head. *Naukratis: Part I (1884–5).* London, 1888.

Pinkerton, John, ed. *A General Collection of the Most Interesting Voyages and Travels in All Parts of the World.* 17 vols. London, 1814.

Plato. *The Dialogues of Plato.* Trans. by Benjamin Jowett. 5 vols. Oxford, 1931.

Pliny. *Selections from the History of the World Commonly Called the Natural History of C. Plinius Secundus.* Trans. by Philemon Holland, ed. by Paul Turner. Carbondale, Ill., 1962.

Plutarch. *Plutarch's Moralia.* Vol. V. Trans. by Frank Cole Babbitt. 14 vols. Cambridge, Mass., 1936.

Pococke, Richard. *A Description of the East, and Some Other Countries.* London, 1743.

Poole, Sophia. *The Englishwoman in Egypt: Letters from Cairo, Written During a Residence There in 1842, 3, & 4.* Philadelphia, 1845.

Prichard, James. *An Analysis of Egyptian Mythology.* London, 1819.

Purchas, Samuel, ed. *Hakluytus Posthumus or Purchas His Pilgrimes Contayning a History of the World in Sea Voyages and Lande Travells by Englishmen and Others.* 20 vols. Glasgow, 1905.

Ralegh, Sir Walter. *The History of the World in Five Books.* 6 vols. Edinburgh, 1920.

Rawlinson, George. *A History of Ancient Egypt.* In *The Works of George Rawlinson.* 2 vols. London, 1881, Boston, 1882.

Ray, John, ed. *A Collection of Curious Travels and Voyages.* 2 vols. London, 1738.

Rhind, Alexander Henry. *Thebes: Its Tombs and Their Tenants Ancient and Present, Including a Record of Excavations in the Necropolis.* London, 1862.

Roberts, David, Reverend George Croby, and William Brockedon. *The Holy Land.* 6 vols. London, 1855.

Rollin, Charles. *The Ancient History of the Egyptians, Carthaginians, Assyrians, Babylonians, Medes and Persians, Grecians and Macedonians.* Trans. by R. Lynam. 8 vols. London, 1829.

Ross, Janet. *Three Generations of Englishwomen.* 2 vols. London, 1888.

Salame, Abraham V. *A Narrative of the Expedition to Algiers in the Year 1816.* London, 1819.

Salt, Henry. *Essay on Dr. Young's and M. Champollion's Phonetic System of Hieroglyphics.* London, 1825.

Sanderson, John. *The Travels of John Sanderson.* In *Works Issued by the Hakluyt Society.* Ed. by Sir William Foster. 2d ser., No. LXVII. London, 1931.

Scot, Reginald. *The Discoverie of Witchcraft.* London, 1584.

Shakespeare, William. *Othello.* In *The Arden Edition of the Works of William Shakespeare.* Ed. by M. R. Ridley. London, 1958.

———. *Shakespeare's Sonnets.* Ed. by A. L. Rowse. London, 1964.

———. *The Tragedy of Anthony and Cleopatra.* In *The Yale Shakespeare.* Ed. by Peter G. Phialas. London, 1955.

Sharp, William. *Life of Percy Bysshe Shelly.* London, 1887.

Sharpe, Samuel. *The History of Egypt from the Earliest Times till the Conquest by the Arabs A.D. 640.* 2 vols. London, 1852.

Shaw, Robert. *Creator and Cosmos.* St. Louis, 1889.

Shaw, Thomas. *Travels, Or Observations Relating to Several Parts of Barbary and the Levant.* Oxford, 1738.

Shelley, Percy Bysshe. *The Poetical Works of Percy Bysshe Shelley.* Ed. by H. Buxton Forman. 2 vols. London, 1886.

Smith, Thomas. *The Wonders of Nature and Art.* 12 vols. London, 1803.

Smith, William. *The Illustrated History of the Bible.* Philadelphia, 1871.

Spenser, Edmund. *The Poetical Works of Edmund Spenser.* Ed. by J. C. Smith. 3 vols. Oxford, 1909.

Strabo. *The Geography of Strabo.* Trans. by Horace Leonard Jones, In *The Loeb Classical Library.* Ed. by T. E. Page, E. Copps, and W. H. D. Rouse. 8 vols. London, 1932.

Stuart, John. *Memoir of the Late Alexander Henry Rhind.* With Vol. V of *Proceedings of the Society of Antiquities of Scotland.* Edinburgh, 1865.

Thomas, William. *The History of Italy (1549).* Ed. by George B. Parks. Ithaca, 1963.

Thornbury, Walter. *Criss-Cross Journeys.* 2 vols. London, 1873.

Tomkins, Reverend Henry G. *The Life and Times of Joseph in the Light of Egyptian Lore.* Vol. XVII of *By-Paths of Bible Knowledge.* London, 1893.

Vallancy, Charles. *An Essay on the Antiquity of the Irish Language.* Dublin, 1772.

Von Hammer-Purgstall, Joseph, trans. *Narrative of Travels in Europe, Asia, and Africa.* London, 1834.

Vyse, Richard Howard. *Operations Carried on at the Pyramids of Gizeh in 1837.* 2 vols. London, 1840.

Walker, Reverend Francis A. *Nine Hundred Miles up the Nile.* London, 1884.

Wall, Charles William. *An Examination of the Ancient Orthography of the Jews with Which Is Incorporated an Essay on Egyptian Hieroglyphs.* London, 1835.

Walloth, Wilhelm. *The King's Treasure House: A Romance of Ancient Egypt.* Trans. by Mary J. Safford. New York, 1886.

Walpole, Robert, ed. *Memoirs Relating to European and Asiatic Turkey, and Other Countries of the East.* London, 1818.

Warburton, William. *The Divine Legation of Moses.* 2 vols. London, 1837–41.

Wathen, George Henry. *Arts, Antiquities and Chronology of Ancient Egypt.* London, 1843.

Webbe, Edward. *Edward Webbe, Chief Master Gunner, His Travailes.* In *Bibliotheca Curiosa.* Ed. by Edmund Goldsmed. Edinburgh, 1885.

Webster, John. *The Displaying of Supposed Witchcraft.* London, 1677.

Wilkinson, Sir John Gardner. *Manners and Customs of the Ancient Egyptians.* 3 vols. London, 1841.

———. *A Popular Account of the Ancient Egyptians.* 2 vols. London, 1854.

———. *Topography of Thebes.* London, 1835.

Wilson, John. *John Wilson's The Cheats.* Ed. by Milton C. Nahm. Oxford, 1935.

———. *The Lost Solar System of the Ancients Discovered.* 2 vols. London, 1852–56.

*The World Displayed; Or a Curious Collection of Voyages and Travels.* 20 vols. London, 1767.

Zincke, F. Barham. *Egypt of the Pharaohs and of the Khedive.* London, 1873.

## B. Periodicals

*Academy* (London)

*American Journal of Archaeology*

*American Quarterly Review*

*Andover Review*

*Annual Report of the Board of Regents of the Smithsonian Institution* (1869)

*Appleton's Popular Science Monthly*

*Archaeologia: Or Miscellaneous Tracts, Relating to Antiquity*

*Archaeological Journal, the British Archaeological Association*

*Arena*

*Athenaeum: Journal of English and Foreign Literature, Science, the Fine Arts, Music and the Drama*

*Atlantic Monthly*

*Baptist Quarterly*

*Belgravia: An Illustrated London Magazine*

*Blackwood's Edinburgh Magazine*

*British Quarterly Review*

*Cambridge Essays*

*Century Magazine*

*Chamber's Edinburgh Journal*

*Chamber's Journal of Popular Literature, Science, and Art*

*Christian Century*

*Christian Examiner and General Review*

*Contemporary Review*

*Critic*

*Edinburgh Philosophical Journal*

*Edinburgh Review, or Critical Journal*

*European Magazine and London Review*

*Foreign Quarterly Review*

*Fraser's Magazine for Town and Country*

*Gentleman's Magazine and Historical Chronicle*

*Harper's Monthly Magazine*

*Harper's New Monthly Magazine*

*Household Words: A Weekly Journal Conducted by Charles Dickens*

*Journal of the Anthropological Institute of Great Britain and Ireland*
*Journal of Egyptian Archaeology*
*Journal of the Royal Geographical Society of London*
*Leisure Hour*
*Littell's Living Age*
*Living Age*
*Monthly Review*
*Nation*
*National Magazine Devoted to Literature, Art, and Religion*
*Nature: A Weekly Illustrated Journal of Science*
*New Englander*
*New England Magazine*
*New Monthly Magazine*
*North American Review*
*North British Review*
*Notes and Queries*
*Penny Magazine of the Society for the Diffusion of Useful Knowledge*
*Philosophical Transactions of the Royal Society of London*
*Proceedings of the Society of Antiquaries of Scotland*
*Prospective Review: A Quarterly Journal of Theology and Literature*
*Quarterly Review*
*Review of Reviews*
*Saturday Review*
*Scientific American Supplement*
*Scribner's Magazine*
(London) *Times Literary Supplement*
*Transactions of the Royal Irish Academy*
*Unitarian Review and Religious Magazine*
*Westminster Review*

## C. Newspapers

*Lloyd's Evening Post and British Chronicle*, Vol. XXI (September 28–30, 1767).
*London Times* (January 26, 1877–October 30, 1884).

M

## II. SECONDARY MATERIALS

### A. Reference Works

Baedeker, Karl. *Egypt: Handbook for Travellers.* 2 vols. London, 1885.

Bateson, Frederick Wilse, ed. *The Cambridge Bibliography of English Literature.* 5 vols. Cambridge, 1941–57.

Boase, Frederick. *Modern English Biography.* 6 vols. London, 1965.

Chambers, Robert. *A Biographical Dictionary of Eminent Scotsmen.* 4 vols. Glasgow, 1835.

Davies, Godfrey, ed. *Bibliography of British History: Stuart Period, 1603–1714.* Oxford, 1928.

Doberer, Kurt Karl. *The Goldmakers: 10,000 Years of Alchemy.* Trans. by E. W. Dicks. London, 1948.

*The Georgian Era.* 4 vols. London, 1834.

Grose, Clyde Leclare. *A Select Bibliography of British History, 1660–1760.* Chicago, 1939.

Pargellis, Stanley, and D. J. Medley, eds. *Bibliography of British History: The Eighteenth Century 1714–1789.* Oxford, 1951.

Read, Conyers, ed. *Bibliography of British History: Tudor Period, 1485–1603.* Oxford, 1959.

Stephen, Leslie, and Sidney Lee, eds. *The Dictionary of National Biography.* 63 vols. and supplements. London, 1885–1900, with later supplements.

### B. Books

Baikie, James. *A Century of Excavation in the Land of the Pharaohs.* London, 1924.

Baker, John Norman Leonard. *A History of Geographical Discovery and Exploration.* London, 1931.

Benson, Edward Frederic. *King Edward VII: An Appreciation.* New York, 1933.

Blunden, Edmund. *Keats's Publisher: A Memoir of John Taylor (1781–1864).* London, 1936.

Breasted, James Henry. *A History of Egypt.* New York, 1905.

Budge, Sir Ernest Alfred Thompson Wallis. *The Egyptian Sudan: Its History and Monuments.* 2 vols. London, 1907.
———. *The Rosetta Stone in the British Museum.* London, 1929.
Cawley, Robert Ralston. *Unpathed Waters: Studies in the Influence of the Voyagers on Elizabethan Literature.* Princeton, 1940.
———. *The Voyagers and Elizabethan Drama.* Boston, 1938.
Ceram, C. W. [Kurt W. Marek]. *Gods, Graves, and Scholars: The Story of Archaeology.* Trans. by E. B. Garside. New York, 1956.
———. *The March of Archaeology.* Trans. by Richard and Clara Winston. New York, 1958.
Chancellor, Edwin Beresford. *The Hell Fire Club.* Vol. IV in *The Lives of the Rakes.* 6 vols. London, 1925.
Chew, Samuel C. *The Crescent and The Rose: Islam and England During the Renaissance.* New York, 1937.
Clark, H. F. *The English Landscape Garden.* London, 1948.
Cohen, Morton Norton. *Rider Haggard: His Life and Works.* London, 1960.
Cottrell, Leonard. *The Mountains of Pharaoh.* New York, 1956.
Curling, Jonathan. *Edward Wortley Montagu, 1713–1776: The Man in the Iron Wig.* New York, 1954.
Daniel, Glyn Edmund. *A Hundred Years of Archaeology.* London, 1952.
———. *The Idea of Prehistory.* Cleveland and New York, 1963.
Davis, Richard Beale. *George Sandys: Poet-Adventurer.* London, 1955.
Disher, Maurice Willson. *Pharaoh's Fool.* London, 1957.
Ebers, Georg. *Richard Lepsius: A Biography.* Trans. by Zoe Dona Underhill. New York, 1887.
Edwards, Edward. *Lives of the Founders of the British Museum.* London, 1870.
Evans, Joan. *A History of the Society of Antiquaries.* Oxford, 1956.
Fakhry, Ahmed. *The Pyramids.* Chicago, 1961.
Gardiner, Sir Alan Henderson. *Egypt of the Pharaohs: An Introduction.* Oxford, 1961.

Gardner, Martin. *Fads and Fallacies in the Name of Science.* New York, 1957.

Gunther, Robert William Theodore. *Early Science in Oxford.* 14 vols. Oxford, 1937.

Hagen, Victor Wolfgang von. *Frederick Catherwood, Architect.* New York, 1950.

Head, Major Francis B. *The Life of Bruce, the African Traveller.* London, 1853.

Heawood, Edward. *A History of Geographical Discovery in the Seventeenth and Eighteenth Centuries.* Cambridge, 1912.

Herold, J. Christopher. *Bonaparte in Egypt.* New York, 1962.

Hotson, Leslie. *Shakespeare's Sonnets Dated and Other Essays.* London, 1949.

Iversen, Erik. *The Myth of Egypt and Its Hieroglyphs in European Tradition.* Copenhagen, 1961.

King, James. *Cleopatra's Needle.* London, 1883.

Jameson, Robert, James Wilson, and Hugh Murray. *Narrative of Discovery and Adventure in Africa.* Edinburgh, 1830.

Manuel, Frank E. *Isaac Newton: Historian.* Cambridge, Mass., 1963.

Martelli, George. *Jemmy Twitcher: A Life of the Fourth Earl of Sandwich, 1718–1792.* London, 1962.

Maspero, Sir Gaston. *History of Egypt, Chaldea, Syria, Babylonia, and Assyria.* Trans. by M. L. McClure. 12 vols. London, 1903–1906.

Mertz, Barbara. *Temples, Tombs and Hieroglyphs: The Story of Egyptology.* New York, 1964.

Michaelis, Adolf Theodor Friedrich. *A Century of Archaeological Discoveries.* Trans. by Bettina Kahnweiler, pref. by Percy Gardner. London, 1908.

Moorehead, Alan. *The Blue Nile.* New York, 1962.

Nicolson, Nigel. *Great Houses of Britain.* New York, 1965.

Piggott, Stuart. *William Stukeley: An Eighteenth-Century Antiquary.* Oxford, 1950.

Tunstall, Brian. *William Pitt, Earl of Chatham.* London, 1938.

Turner, Ralph E. *James Silk Buckingham, 1786–1855: A Social Biography.* New York, 1934.

Waite, Arthur Edward. *The Secret Tradition in Alchemy*. London, 1926.

Ward, A. W., and A. R. Waller. *The Cambridge History of English Literature*. 15 vols. New York, 1912.

Whates, Henry Richard. *The Life and Times of King Edward VII*. 5 vols. London, 1910.

Wilson, Erasmus. *Cleopatra's Needle*. London, 1878.

Wilson, John A. *Signs & Wonders upon Pharaoh: A History of American Egyptology*. Chicago, 1964.

Wood, Alexander, and Frank Oldham. *Thomas Young: Natural Philosopher, 1773–1829*. Cambridge, 1954.

### Selected Articles and Essays

Babbitt, Frank Cole. "Introduction to Isis and Osiris." In Vol. V of *Plutarch's Moralia*. 14 vols. Cambridge, Mass., and London, 1836.

Dannenfeldt, Karl H. "Egypt and Egyptian Antiquities in the Renaissance," *Studies in the Renaissance*, Vol. VI (1959), 7–27.

Dawson, Warren Royal. "Anastasi, Sallier, and Harris and Their Papyri," *JEA*, Vol. XXXV (December, 1949), 158–66.

———. "The First Egyptian Society," *JEA*, Vol. XXIII (December, 1937), 259–60.

———. "Pettigrew's Demonstrations upon Mummies: A Chapter in the History of Egyptology," *JEA*, Vol. XX (1934), 170–82.

Foster, Sir William. "Introduction," *The Travels of John Sanderson in the Levant 1584–1602*. In *Works Issued by the Hakluyt Society*. 2d ser., Vol. LXVII (1931), ix–xli.

Parks, George B. "Introduction," in William Thomas. *The History of Italy (1549)*. Ithaca, 1963.

# Index